Dedication

There are good friends, there are great friends, and then:
there are COWBOY FRIENDS!

Thanks to all my wonderful cowboy friends for:
Answering endless and repetitive questions about cows.
Bringing me firewood, Christmas trees and manure!
Fixing fences
Taking me to rodeos, out to lunch and on many a ranch tour.
Suggesting great stories for my books, setting up interviews for my books and taking me
to the ranch for the interview!
Sharing their ranch life, their knowledge and expertise and opening their homes to my
family and friends from around the world!

Vic and Jamie Howell
Scott and Victoria Westlake
Clay and Danielle Rogers
Ryan and Cassandra Manifee
Dave and Karen Myers
Barry and Sherri Guillet
Everett and Leah Ashurst

Plus, all my adorable little cowboys and cowgirls:
Kathryn, Rebecca, Lauren, Samantha, Thomas, Elizabeth, Benjamin and Matthew!

ISBN: 978-0-9858952-6-6

Cover photo:
Unless otherwise noted, all photos are public domain, found online

For more information or questions, contact unbreakabledolls@gmail.com, to order multiple copies of any of Julie's books, email randi.diskin@gmail.com

Layout and Design:
Randi Diskin

Saints & Scoundrels

Colorful Characters of Arizona

Julie McDonald

Significant Places Mentioned in These Stories

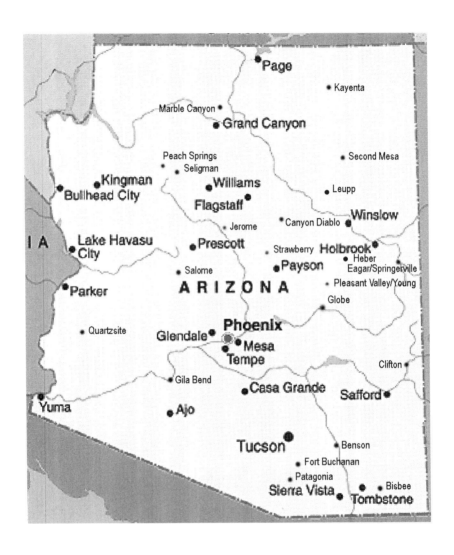

TABLE OF CONTENTS

Climax Jim of Clifton 1876-1921

If there ever was a lovable outlaw it would have to be Rufus "Climax Jim" Nephew of Clifton, so named because his favorite chew brand was *Climax Chewing Tobacco*.

Born in Washington D.C., he arrived in Arizona as a teen. He launched his criminal career at the age of 17. His first arrest came after he tried to sell a dozen steers he had stolen to a slaughterhouse in Winslow. That same night he tunneled out of the adobe jail using a pocketknife.

Rufus "Climax Jim" Nephew, circa 1890's

A few months later, on the 4th of July, he stole a horse and was tracked down by Gila County Sheriff, John "Rim Rock" Thompson, near Pleasant Valley. The first night after capture they camped in the woods and Climax Jim was chained to a post with leg irons. He managed to break one of the links and escaped on foot. 50 miles later he was captured just south of Globe. He was then hauled to the jail in Globe. This time it took him a couple of months, but he managed to dig his way out of jail using a spoon. He loosened the mortar around the bricks and removed them one by one until the hole was large enough for him to crawl through. For this accomplishment he was dubbed, "The Spoon Kid."

By now, every newspaper in the Arizona Territory- and there were lots of them- was keeping all of the citizens thoroughly entertained with Climax Jim's antics.

He alternated between stealing cows, stealing horses and getting caught. During one of his stints in jail, the Sheriff thought he needed a bath. He took Climax Jim out to the horse trough. He handed him a bar of soap and a brush and just as Climax Jim was getting ready to step into the trough he spotted a nice looking horse. He was off in a flash and stark naked, he rode out of town. The shocked residents of Eagar and Springerville would not soon forget their own version of "Lady Godiva."

When he wasn't digging his way out of jails, he escaped by picking locks. He was a masterful lock and safe picker. He was a man of many talents! One night he told a sheriff after being locked in the cell that he would be out by morning. The next morning, the sheriff arrived to find Climax Jim, grinning from ear to ear, seated at his desk, in his office chair, sipping coffee.

Climax Jim would later brag that he had "busted out of every jail in the Territory" except the famed "Hell Hole," the Yuma Territorial Prison where he had spent one year.

He was indicted by a grand jury 5 different times, and all five times he was able to talk his way out of it. The prosecuting attorneys finally gave up.

He did run a legitimate retail business, a butcher shop in Clifton. A butcher shop was a nice compliment to his cattle rustling business.

A favorite story, and the one for which he is best known, is his trial in 1907 for altering and then cashing a check. The altered check was "EXHIBIT A" at this trial and was in the courtroom on the prosecuting attorney's desk. While his lawyer and the prosecuting attorney were arguing a point before the judge, Climax Jim reached over, picked up the check and added it to his mouthful of chew. Without any evidence, a mistrial was declared and the case was dismissed. On his way out of the courtroom, Climax Jim spit the chew and the remains of the check into the judge's personal spittoon.

Somehow, during his very busy life, Climax Jim managed to get married and father a child. He, his wife Gertrude and baby, left the Arizona Terri-

Climax Jim, circa early 1900's

tory around 1910. He apparently gave up his life of crime and started his own business as a well driller near San Diego. Three more children were added to the family before his tragic death in 1921 at the age of 45. He apparently died when some scaffolding he was working on collapsed.

Looking dignified and like the epitome of a law abiding citizen in the Arizona Territory, circa 1907.

LARCENA PENNINGTON 1837-1913

A common fear among the immigrants traveling west, especially women, was the fear of Indians. In reality, the chance of having an unpleasant experience with the Native Americans was rare. Any atrocities committed against white settlers were greatly exaggerated and widely told. However, violence committed by white soldiers and settlers against the Natives were rarely told.

Larcena Pennington, circa 1870's

Larcena's experience was what every woman feared. The Pennington family had picked a bad time to move to the Arizona Territory, which at that time before the Civil War was considered part of the enormous New Mexico Territory. When they arrived from Nashville, Tennessee via Texas, they were the first family of United States citizenship to settle in what would become the Arizona Territory. The Pennington family consisted of father, Elias, and his 12 children, 4 boys and 8 girls. Their mother, Julia Ann, had died during their time in Texas. The Pennington family was on a wagon train headed to California. When their animals succumbed to exhaustion, the family was forced to settle south of what is today, the small town of Benson, Arizona along the San Pedro River.

In 1859, at age 22, Larcena met and married John Page. Their wedding on Christmas Eve, was the first for United States settlers in Tucson, then, just an adobe village.

Three months later, Larcena was with John at his lumber camp high in the Santa Rita Mountains south of Tucson. Also at the camp were William Randall and Mercedes Quiroz, the 11 year old adopted daughter of the lumber company's owner.

On the morning of March 16, 1860, John Page left camp to attend to lumber business and William Randall went deer hunting. The first sign of trouble was a dog barking, then a scream from Mercedes. Larcena looked up from her laundry and saw the Apaches running toward her. Her account was published in the Missouri Republican on May 8, 1860: "Having a six shooter in my hand, I turned to fire at them but they were already so close that before I could pull the trigger they had rushed upon me and seized the weapon." The Apaches stormed the camp, looted it and captured Larcena and Mercedes. As the Apaches marched them off, Larcena and Mercedes began tearing bits of cotton cloth from their dresses to leave a trail. When the Apaches saw what they were doing, they put an end to it. All day they walked, 16 miles through rough terrain. At the end of the day, Larcena was exhausted and could go no further. The Apaches decided she was a liability and made the decision to kill her. In her account of that terrifying day Larcena writes, "They striped me of my clothing, including my shoes and left me with a single garment. They thrust their lances at me, inflicting 11 wounds in my body, threw me over a ledge of rocks, some 16-18 feet high and hurled large stones after me. Then they left me, supposing that I must die." Larcena then slipped into unconsciousness. She awoke to voices, including her husband's on the trail above. "Here it is boys!" She heard them say. They had found the trail and the mark of her shoes, now worn by an Apache. Larcena called out to them, but she was so weak they didn't hear her. Again she slipped into unconsciousness. When she awoke again, she applied snow to her wounds. She was weak from blood loss, barefoot, and wearing only a thin petticoat. She began the long trek home. After only one day her feet were so bloody she was forced to crawl.

She described the desperate situation she was in, "Sometimes, after crawling up a steep ledge, laboring hard for half a day, I would lose my grip and slide down lower than the place from which I started." To survive, she ate grass and snow. At night she would sleep in holes she dug in the sand. In the morning she would wait for the warmth of the sun before setting out again. Her fair skin, never exposed to sunlight before, was badly sun burned.

After almost two weeks Larcena reached a recently deserted camp. The campfire was still smoldering. She got it going again and with a small bit of flour that had spilled on the ground she made "bread." It was the first real food she had since the kidnapping. She heard and saw workmen employed by her husband but was too weak to call out to them. When the workmen finally stumbled upon her she was unrecognizable. The men ran for their guns. Her skin was burned and peeling. Her hair was matted with dirt and blood. She was so emaciated she looked like a skeleton. She had multiple bruises and gaping wounds. Her lips were stretched so tightly across her jaw; her teeth were visible through them.

Larcena's survival and return to her husband through this two-week period can only be described as miraculous. How did she survive the elements, her injuries, and lack of food? Why was she not attacked an eaten by coyotes, wolves, mountain lions or bears? Why she didn't fall ill to hypothermia is also a mystery.

The 16 mile trek also exhausted little Mercedes. She was small and light enough to carry, which the Apaches did. She was later returned, basically unharmed, in a prisoner swap.

After returning to a somewhat normal life, Larcena's troubles weren't over. Soldiers had abandoned the Arizona Territory to fight in the Civil War. Her husband, John Page was killed two years later by Apaches. Her father Elias and two of her brothers were also killed by Apaches. Her sister Ann died of malaria and her sister Ellen died of pneumonia. Larcena and her baby, Mary Ann contracted the dreaded smallpox.

The Pennington family had had enough of the Arizona Territory and moved back to Texas. Yet Larcena stayed. In 1870, at age 33 she remarried lawyer and judge, William Scott. Their wedding announcement was published in the Weekly Arizonian:

> Wm. Scott, Esq., of the firm Lee and Scott of this place, after having withstood the dangers and hardships of about twelve years of frontier life, and reached a standard of prosperity which most men might envy, was last week--- not killed by Apaches, as the reader might suppose, but on the

contrary, quite otherwise---united in marriage to a most excellent lady, daughter of the late Mr. Pennington, a lady who, individually and in connection with her family, has already figured prominently in the history of the early settler in Arizona.

William and Larcena Scott had two children, William and Georgie. She remained in Tucson until she died at age 76 in 1913. She was a founding member of the Congregational Church of Tucson and president of the fledgling Arizona Historical Society. At the end of her life she was described as a sweet natured, happy, tall and dignified woman with white hair. Pennington Street in downtown Tucson is named in honor of the Pennington family.

Charles Sterling

Sterling may have been his last name but it certainly wasn't a description of his character. In December of 1884, Charles Sterling thought he could use some beef to help get him through the winter. He didn't own any cattle, so he helped himself to a heifer owned by Benjamin Franklin Coppell. Coppell was running cattle not far from Sedona. Sterling butchered the heifer, and then cut off the ears with the identifying ear notch and the brand. Sterling congratulated himself on this brilliant act as he hoisted the meat onto his horse and headed home. He wasn't nearly as brilliant as he thought he was. As he headed back to his cabin 12 miles up Oak Creek Canyon, the meat leaked a steady trail of blood. Since it had been snowing, the blood left a clear trail in the freshly fallen snow.

When the remains of the heifer were discovered, a sheriff's posse headed up by Jim Thompson set out to apprehend the cattle rustler. Cattle rustling was a serious offense in the West and justice was often served swiftly on a hanging tree at the end of a rope. The posse followed the clear trail of blood all the way up Oak Creek Canyon to Dave Clark's cabin where Sterling was planning to hole up for the winter.

The posse found much more than the butchered beef. They found a purse full of counterfeit money along with a counterfeit printing press. Sterling was arrested immediately and taken to Prescott, the territorial capital for trial. In the spring of 1885 Judge Goodman sentenced Sterling to two years in the Yuma Territorial Prison, an absolutely dreadful place.

Sterling Springs, Sterling Pass and Sterling Canyon are all named for him.

Richard Wilson

We might not have heard the name Richard Wilson had it not been for Charles Sterling. Sterling had been sitting in jail in Prescott awaiting trial for a good six months.

In June of 1885, the men in the posse who had found and captured Charles Sterling were called upon to testify at the trial. Prescott was a long way from Sedona and Oak Creek Canyon and would take a good two days to get there on horseback.

Richard Wilson saw this as a good opportunity to get his high powered rifle fixed. The site was a bit off. The men agreed to take it under one condition. "Richard, you got to promise you won't go messing with that big ole' bear you been after. That small caliber rifle would do nothing to that bear. You promise now."

Richard Wilson promised, but when he spotted the huge Grizzly it was too tempting. He shot the bear. The bear turned and came toward Wilson. Richard Wilson climbed the nearest tree, an Arizona Cyprus, but the bear reached up with its giant claws and pulled Wilson out of the tree.

Wilson's partially eaten body was discovered a few days later. The claw marks on his boots, which had been pulled off, told the story. His small caliber rifle was found nearby, but the knife he always carried was missing.

30 years later, Jim James and Mark Ferrell were on a hunting expedition in a remote canyon when they discovered the skeleton of an enormous Grizzly bear. The bear measured 6' 6". As they examined the skeleton more closely they discovered Richard Wilson's missing hunting knife. The bear had carried it as long as it had lived. The last Grizzly bear in Arizona was killed near Williams at White Horse Lake in 1926.

Wilson Mountain, Wilson Canyon, and Wilson Trail (one of the most popular hiking trails in the Sedona area) are all named for Richard Wilson.

Sarah Bowman 1813-1866

Sarah Bowman was larger than life. Sarah Bowman was also larger than every woman and most of the men at that time. A giantess of a woman she was over 6 feet tall and 200 pounds. She had fiery red hair and a fiery temper to go with it. She was fair skinned with bright blue eyes, possibly of Celtic descent. The 200 pounds was not fat but muscle and whoa to the unfortunate man who thought he could whip her. Her insurance policy was not one, but two pistols she carried around her waist.

Sarah was most often found in the company of various military operations. Officially, she was the cook and/or laundress. Unofficially, she had many roles. She tended the wounded, brought coffee and food to the men while they protected the walls during artillery fire. Once while serving the men, bullets passed right through her hat and another time hit the bread tray she was carrying. Sarah was known to also pick up a musket or a rifle and join the fight.

Sarah was intensely loyal to the country, the military forces and her commanding officers. She saw herself as a helper. Since she was caring for many of the needs of the men through cooking, laundry and cleaning she added one more service. When the outfit wasn't engaged in active battle, Sarah often operated a brothel.

She was married a number of times to military men, which allowed her to remain in military service. When one of her husbands died she was told she could not continue with the squadron unless she was married and "mustered in" as a laundress.

"All right Major," Sarah replied, "I'll marry the whole squadron and YOU thrown in, but what [where the troops go] I go along." Sarah then mounted the nearest horse and rode past the line of soldiers shouting, "Who wants a wife with 15,000 dollars and the biggest leg in Mexico? Come me beauties, don't all speak at once! Who is the lucky man?"

The soldiers stood in shocked silence. Finally, a soldier by the name of Davis stepped forward. Sarah's comments about the pleasures that awaited the lucky man will not be repeated here. The marriage didn't last. Sarah spotted another soldier whose "gigantic proportions" were more to her liking. Davis was tossed out of her tent and the new man was in.

In addition to operating a brothel, Sarah sometimes ran an orphanage as well. Usually the operations ran consecutively but sometimes she was running both at the same time at the same place. At one time Sarah was caring for five orphaned children, all with the first name of "Skinner."

In 1852, Sarah now 39, had another new husband, 24 year old Albert Bowman. Sarah and Albert moved to Yuma for a time. Sarah described Yuma as, "separated from Hell by one thin sheet of sandpaper." Later, they moved to Tucson where they operated a boarding house. En route to Tucson they passed the site of the Oatman Massacre. They stopped and moved the Oatman family's remains to more permanent graves along the Gila Trail. Earlier that year in 1856, Olive Oatman was in Fort Yuma after five years of captivity. Sarah had taken her in and cared for her. Sarah and Olive became very good friends.

Sarah and Albert had one more stint with the army in 1857. They sold their property in Tucson and accompanied the First Dragoons to Sonoita Creek where Fort Buchanan was established. While there, Sarah ran a saloon and brothel in nearby Patagonia.

At age 49 with the Civil War raging, Sarah still wanted more than anything to accompany the troops. Her marriage to Albert by this time had dissolved and she was denied. Sarah was heartbroken and died a few years later in 1866 at age 53, possibly from a spider bite. She was given full military honors and buried at Fort Yuma. Sarah Bowman was the only woman so honored.

In 1890, 160 graves at Fort Yuma were moved to the Presidio National Cemetery in San Francisco. Sarah was included and went for the last time "with the troops."

GEORGE KIRK AND THE NAVAJO CODE TALKERS

My mother, Cecile Benson, came to Arizona in 1942 to work as a nurse at the Navajo Ordinance Depot in Bellemont, west of Flagstaff. Besides housing ammunition for the war effort, the town was also home to many Austrian prisoners of war. My mother, being half Austrian, was especially kind to these men. They were so appreciative of her care and kindness that they made her numerous beautiful wood carvings, which I still have today.

After the war, my mother continued working as a nurse at the Navajo Ordinance Depot where she made many friends. One of her very good friends was a Navajo man by the name of George Kirk. As a child I remember my mother baking bread or some other delicious treat to deliver to and visit with George and his wife, Beatrice. They had two beautiful daughters, Joan and Gloria who were a little older then I but we all attended Flagstaff High School. The Kirk family lived in a cinder block home, with a neat and tidy yard and many Navajo artifacts in their home.

I remember on one of those trips my mother explaining to me that George Kirk was a very important man. He had a very important job in World War II. I didn't understand until I was an adult what that job was. George Kirk was a Navajo Code Talker.

During World War II the Japanese were breaking all of our codes. Our messages were being intercepted. Navy ships were sunk; secret attacks were discovered, and then thwarted. The United States was in serious trouble.

Philip Johnston was living in Los Angeles in the early 1940's at the start of World War II. He had an idea. Johnston was 4 years old in 1896 when his parents came to the Navajo Reservation near Leupp, Arizona as the first protestant missionaries. Young Philip's playmates were Navajo children and he quickly learned the very difficult, and at that time unwritten, Navajo language. He became so proficient that at age 9 he accompanied his father and Navajo leaders for an important meeting in

Washington D.C. with President Theodore Roosevelt. 9 year old Philip was the Navajo-English translator between Navajo leaders and President Roosevelt.

In April 1942, 4 months after the bombing of Pearl Harbor, Philip Johnston proposed an idea to USMC Major, James E. Jones at Camp Elliot in San Diego. He proposed to use Navajos speaking their own language to send important military messages. Johnston had maintained friendships with Navajos whom he had grown up with. He offered to bring 4 of them who were working in the Los Angeles shipyards in for a demonstration. General Clayton Vogel heard about the demonstration and attended the event. The Navajo men, fluent in both Navajo and English, were divided up into 2 groups and put in 2 separate rooms at opposite ends of the building where field phones had been installed. They were given a message in English, which had to be translated into Navajo and sent in Navajo over the wire. The Navajos in the other room received the message in Navajo and then translated it back into English. The message was translated PERFECTLY!

General Vogel and Major Jones and other observers were enthusiastic but their superiors in Washington were hesitant. They were reluctant to entrust the entire military operations in the Pacific Theatre to Indians from an Arizona Reservation. Desperation can sometimes lead people to take risks and the Americans were desperate. They had been trying to take one small, but very important island. All previous attempts had failed as the Japanese had intercepted every message and an-

Technical Sergeant Philip Johnston in front of the El Pueblo Motel on Route 66 in Flagstaff, Arizona. Johnston used the motel as his "base camp" for Navajo Code Talker recruitment trips to the Navajo Reservation.

ticipated their attacks. As an experiment, the Code Talkers were used and the Japanese were unable to intercept the message and the island was taken. Initially 200 Code Talkers were requested, but the military would only start with 30, one dropped out but 29 completed the program. Philip Johnston was 50 at the time but given the job of Staff Sergeant in charge of Navajo Code Talker recruitment and training. It wasn't long before the military could see how well this was working and began the recruitment of 200.

The Navajos were not only accurate, they were fast! What used to take hours to transmit, now took only minutes. They not only used their native language but a code within the language. Some words were coded for something familiar. The Navajos do not have a word for grenade, so potato was used. A fighter plane became a hummingbird and an observation plane was an owl, a Dive Bomber was a Chicken Hawk, a Torpedo plane was a swallow. An aircraft carrier was a bird carrier and a submarine was an iron fish. Other important names of islands, cities and military bases were coded by spelling the word with the first letter of a Navajo word. All these different things the Navajos had to memorize. For them, coming from an oral culture and tradition where they had learned histories, clan names, genealogies and ceremonies, without ever writing anything down, memorization was easy and natural.

It is not an exaggeration to say that the Navajo Code talkers saved thousands of lives and shortened World War II. There are some that maintain that without the aid of the Navajo Code Talkers America might have been defeated by the Japanese.

In addition to sending coded messages, they were also considered enlisted men and were called upon to fight as well. 13 of the 400 code talkers were killed in battle.

After the war ended the code talkers were instructed not to talk about what they did in the war. There was thought their service might be needed again in a future conflict. They returned

Pfc. George Kirk (right) and Cpl. Henry Bahe, Jr.

December 1943, serving in Bougainville. Front row, left to right: Pvt. Earl Johnny, Pvt. Kee Etsicitty, Pvt. John V. Goodluck, and PFC David Jordon, Rear row, left to right: Pvt. Jack C. Morgan, Pvt. George H. Kirk, Pvt. Tom H. Jones, and Cpl. Henry Bahe, Jr.

to the reservation and resumed their lives. It was not until 1969 that the military revealed the important job they did. More and more interest has developed as people learn about this incredible story and the tremendous contribution of the Navajo Code Talkers.

In 2001, President George W. Bush awarded the original 29 Code Talkers the Gold Congressional Medal of Honor. Only 5 were still alive to receive it. Surviving family members of the other Code Talkers received the medals. All other Navajo Code Talkers or their family members, nearly 400 were given the Silver Congressional Medal of Honor. President Bush said, "They brought honor to their nation and victory to their country." George Kirk died in 1999 and family members received the medal.

Today, there are more Navajos serving in the United States Military than any other tribe.

For more information:
Wind Talkers is a movie that was made about the Navajo Code Talkers, available on DVD
Navajo Weapon: The Navajo Code Talker by Sally McClain, 2001
Two Ways in the Desert by Bernice Johnston, 1972, wife of Philip
The Burger King Restaurant in Kayenta, Arizona has a fabulous display about the Navajo Code Talkers

I found this story so fascinating I hope to write a short eBook in 2016 about Philip Johnston and the Navajo Code Talkers.

JOHN SHAW

It was almost midnight on Friday, April 7, 1905 in the railroad town of Winslow, in the Arizona Territory. Two strangers came down Third Street, also known as "Saloon Row" and into the Wigwam Saloon. They were well groomed, nicely dressed in suits with felt hats and boots. The two strangers were in their early to mid-twenties.

The two men went up to the bar and ordered a glass of whisky each. While the bartender was pouring the drinks, the taller, red haired, fair skinned John Shaw, nudged his companion, short, dark haired William Smith and gestured to the dice table where silver dollars were being used instead of chips.

Most of the silver dollars were in a pile in front of Frank Ketchum and Hashknife cowboy, Lucien Creswell. Shaw pulled out a gun from his coat and strode over to the table. "Okay gents, keep your hands in sight and nothing will happen. You don't and----" his voice trailed off with an ominous threat. Shaw and Smith loaded up their pockets with as many silver dollars as they could carry and took off into the night. By the time lawmen had been alerted and arrived, the robbers had disappeared.

Finally, a telltale trail of silver dollars led the lawmen to the railroad tracks. Supposing the men had jumped a slow moving freight train, authorities contacted Ed Henderson, Sheriff of Coconino County in Flagstaff and Navajo County Sheriff C. I. "Chet" Houck from Winslow. The sheriffs then got a tip that two men answering the description of the robbers had got off near Canyon Diablo at the trading post owned and operated by Fred Volz. Canyon Diablo lies about 25 miles west, halfway between Winslow and Flagstaff. Volz was in the process of informing the sheriffs that the two suspects had been hanging around when the two appeared.

"Just a minute," Houck shouted to them. "We're officers and we want to look you fellers over."

"Nobody searches us!" called out the shorter man, Smith. John Shaw then reached for his gun and a gunfight ensued which lasted for less than

30 seconds. 21 bullets were fired at close range; the men were never more than 6 feet apart. There were 3 hits and 18 misses! In the end, Houck was slightly wounded, Smith was hit in the leg and John Shaw was dead, with a bullet to his head. How they all weren't killed remained a mystery to everyone, including the survivors.

Sheriff Houck then asked Fred Volz for two things. The first was a coffin to bury John Shaw. Fred Volz kept a supply of pine coffins for Navajos at his trading post and for situations such as this. The other thing he asked for was a Kodak. He wanted a photo so he could make identification of the dead man. A Kodak was given him, but without flash powder there was not enough light for a photograph to be taken.

24 hours later news of the shooting reached the Wigwam Saloon where cowboys from the Hashknife outfit were in town whooping it up on a Saturday night in Winslow. They were quickly getting rip-roaring drunk. The cowboys didn't like Sheriff Houck. It wasn't Chet Houck personally, it stemmed from years of hatred of his brother, Jim Houck, who seemed to always be present at various hangings involving stock thieves (Jim Houck is the cowboy on the front cover of the book, sitting cross legged on the far right with the long hair).

One of the cowboys asserted, "It must have been a bushwhack. Never was a Houck born who wasn't a rope fiend  or a back shooter. That he shot this feller in the side of the head shows he sneaked up on him." Another cowboy, Sam Case interjected, "Come to recollect, didn't them two fellers buy drinks at the bar and pay for them?" The bartender confirmed it was true. Case went on, "I'll wager a coon skin that dirty Houck didn't give that feller a drink before he was planted. We should go down to Canyon Diablo, dig him up, and give him a snort, poor feller."

More cowboys approved of the idea including J.D. Rogers, Hashknife wagon boss. More whisky was consumed and then a train whistle coming from the east signaled their departure. Rogers called out, "There's our iron hoss, let's go!"

Almost forgetting the purpose of the trip, someone remembered to get whiskey and each cowboy grabbed at least one bottle. 25 left the saloon, but only 15 made it on the train including; Sam Case, Lucien Creswell, J.D. Rogers, Tom Hesser, Young Marley, Pete Pemberton, Frank Ketchum, Ezra Haynes, Bill Campbell, Osmer Flake and Jack Le Baron.

Although they had remembered 20 bottles of whiskey for the deceased, no one had thought to bring a shovel. When they disembarked at the Canyon Diablo Trading Post, they woke Fred Volz with the request for one. Fred Volz, up the night before with the shooting, was not happy. "As long as you are going to do this, you no goods," he told them, "take this Kodak along and make some pictures. Might be light enough to get some, time you have him out of the ground. Chet Houck wants pictures to see if he can find out who the dead man really is."

The cowboys then trooped up to boot hill and sat around drinking for a while before they took on the serious task of digging up the deceased.

As the sun rose over the eastern tip of the Painted Desert, Shaw was reveled in his pine box. He looked natural, like he was taking a nap, an amiable grin on his lips. The cowboys crowded around in utter silence. It was no longer a joking expedition. Nobody was drunk anymore. Something about the way the dead man looked struck home. Many of the men were the same age. Many had left Texas or other places on the run from

the law. It could have been them in that casket, or a brother or a fellow cowboy, or a friend. It was a lark when they left the Wigwam, but now there were few dry eyes among them.

Wagon boss Rogers finally broke the spell. "Let's get him out. Now I am glad I came. Let's give him a drink and put him away proper. Somebody can say a prayer, which wasn't done when they shoved him into that hole." Rigor mortis had set in. Bill

Campbell and Sam Case dropped into the grave and lifted him upward to reaching hands. They propped him against the white picket fence of another luckless man's grave who had missed his mark. Then they gave him his last drink, pouring the whiskey between tight teeth. They lowered him into the grave, along with the empty bottle of whiskey, and a prayer was said by a tough and hardened cowboy.

During the entire escapade one of the cowboys, unnoticed, used the Kodak, snapping six photos. Back at the trading post, Fred Volz unloaded the Kodak and handed the film to Creswell with instructions to give it to Sheriff Houck. On the way back to Winslow, Sam Case, still angry at Chet Houck for being Jim Houck's brother, took the film from Creswell saying, "Houck ain't gonna get no pictures." Case then kept the roll for a month and finally gave them to an attorney

4 of the 6 photos. Shaw got some help with his last belly full of whiskey from the Hashknife Cowboys.

in Winslow, "Judge" Burbidge. In time they passed on to Burbidge's son, Ted. Ted gave five of the photos to Gladwell Richardson, who then wrote a piece for Arizona Highways in 1963. Ted kept the sixth photo, the one of the cowboys pouring whiskey into John Shaw's mouth. It disappeared four years after his death in 1955.

EPILOGUE

William Smith was later identified as William Evans. He had been in prison previously for armed robbery in 1897. He was treated at the Santa Fe Hospital in Winslow for his injuries in the gun battle. He then stood trial in October of 1905. He pleaded guilty to robbery and was sentenced to 15 years in the dreaded Yuma Territorial Prison. He served 9 years and was released with a pardon. He never revealed the true identity of John Shaw.

CLARA PENNY 1897-1970

Clara and Joshua walked quietly to the truck, both deep in thought. With the news the Doc had given them, their worst fears had been confirmed. They knew Joshua's lungs had been damaged when he was exposed to nerve gas from the Germans during World War 1. Now in addition, he had been diagnosed with Tuberculosis. With a diagnosis of tuberculosis came the certainty that they would have to move.

A mix of fear and sorrow came over Clara. She was one of 14 children, including 3 sets of twins. Her family had been in Ludlow, Ohio since the Revolutionary War. How far would the Pennys have to go to get to a drier climate?

Clara standing with Lahoma (right) and Joe (left) in 1925. All photos in this story are courtesy of Dave Penny.

With tears and sadness, Joshua and Clara packed up and headed southwest to Healdton, Oklahoma. It was shortly after their arrival that their first baby was born. They did what many people did in that era; they named their baby girl Lahoma, after their new state, Oklahoma.

Fifteen months later, a baby boy arrived who they named Joe. Joshua's health limited him from working as much as he would have liked. His trade was a well driller and his war buddy and best friend, Gus Tschuor, worked for both of them. Gus would prove to be the best possible friend, helping the family his entire life. After

The cabin in Yuma where Clara checked for rattlers every day before the kids were able to go play outside.

two years it became apparent that Oklahoma was not working out. Joshua was not getting better, the air was simply too humid in Oklahoma. They would have to move further west.

You can't get any drier, or any hotter than Yuma, Arizona! Wells were needed there too. So the family and Gus packed

The family's truck outside the Strawberry Schoolhouse during their first winter, 1928. It is the oldest standing schoolhouse in Arizona.

up and moved once again. They had not been in Yuma long when Joshua became so ill he was hospitalized at the Veterans Administration Hospital in Tucson. It was there, while in the hospital and recuperating that Joshua read Zane Grey's new book, "Under the Tonto Rim". Captivated by Grey's description of the Mogollon Rim, Joshua knew he had to go there.

The family packed up once again, and headed to Strawberry, Arizona. For a time, they lived in the old, one room schoolhouse. Joshua then began

The cabin with the chimney that Clara helped move stones for while pregnant, circa 1929.

the difficult work of building a cabin. Clara, along with neighbor, Bob Peach, was his main source of help. Clara, 8 1/2 months pregnant, carried all the stones up from the creek-bed for the fireplace. Two weeks after the cabin was complete, Clara gave birth to another boy, Billy Ray.

Billy grew up to play college football and became a Drug Enforcement Agency Officer.

Their time in Pine was filled with adventure! Lahoma wrote about her memories:

That first summer in Strawberry we were allowed to hunt squirrels. We would take them home and mother would fry them. Sometimes stew or pot pie. We jerked and canned a lot of venison there. Also we would pull meat up in the attic with a rope in winter when it was cool. Mother used lye to make soap; I even had my hair washed with that yellow soap. I remember gathering manzanita berries and wild grapes for jelly.

I remember mountain lions screaming at night. I'd be so scared I couldn't get up to use the pot, called a bedchamber by some people. I'd cover my head and be scared to death.

A short time after we moved to the cabin (that Clara carried the stones for) we were taken to Pine to Etta Fuller's place to spend the night. The next morning before school, Dad came for Joe and me and took us home. Daddy said, "Guess what we have at our house?" Joe answered him, "A coyote in the trap?" Daddy replied, "No, something better, you have a new brother." Sure enough, there was Billy, our baby brother. Dr. Rissor had come from Payson that night and delivered him with Etta Fuller's help. Etta was a midwife and she stayed a night or so with mother. Mother had told me we were getting a baby. I finally caught on when Celeste Patterson and some of the ladies were giving her a shower and there were baby things. Joe never caught on. He was disappointed it wasn't a coyote in the trap.

I remember sitting out front on the warm summer evenings. When the insects bothered us we burned a dry, cow dung patty, which repelled them. Daddy played the harmonica and we would sing and talk. We had a wind up Victrola and some records. Later, we got a battery radio and listened to "Amos and Andy". The Great Depression was on now. Don't you know we were tired and ready for bed after washing baby diapers and clothes outside? Boil in pot, scrub on washboard and in tubs then hang on the clothesline."

Lahoma goes on to remember a frightening time when the creek flooded:

We stood on the Pine side and our parents on the Strawberry side. Couldn't hear each other, the creek was rushing so loud so we put notes in bottles and threw them across. The population in the Strawberry Valley then was about 30. They told us kids to go back to Pine and stay with friends. Each day we came back, but the creek was running too strong.

Finally, they threw a heavy rope across a tree and made a pulley. With an adult taking one small child at a time on their laps, they moved all the children safely across the rushing creek.

In addition to all of this, Clara did odd jobs, kept a garden and chickens, and shot game in the forest and did as much canning as she could to get them through the winter. As much as Joshua and Clara loved Pine and Strawberry, the climate at 6,500 feet elevation was too cold for Joshua's failing health. Reluctantly, they returned to Yuma.

Gus "carried" Joshua over the next few years. Gus would eventually pay for Lahoma to go to Nursing School. They started up a homestead where Clara continued her hard work, planting a garden and raising chickens. Clara recalled before the children were allowed to go outside in the morning, she went first with her 410 shotgun and checked all around the house and under the porch looking for deadly rattlesnakes. In one summer alone she killed 10 rattlers!

In 1936, Joshua at age 41 finally succumbed to the nerve gas damage and tuberculosis. Clara was now left with three growing children, 15, 14 and 7. There was nothing like we have today such as welfare, food stamps, or Social Security for widows and dependent children. You were simply left to try to survive. Many people split up their families and sent children to live with other relatives. Clara did everything she could think of to support herself and her children. She took in boarders and did laundry and ironing. She also cleaned houses for the wealthier people in Yuma. Gus continued helping the family as well.

Another friend, Judge Kelly, knew of her plight and offered her a job as a clerk in the Superior Court. Clara knew nothing of this type of work and her grandson Dave Penny said, "She just blustered her way through."

One day Clara looked across the parking lot to the Yuma County Jail and figured she could get a better job there at a higher wage. It wasn't long before Clara Penny was the Deputy Sheriff of Yuma County! When they needed help in California's Imperial County next door, Clara could be the acting deputy sheriff of that county as well.

Clara (center) with the Yuma County Sheriff's Department in the 1940's.

It was her job to serve papers, arrest offenders and transport prisoners. She served as the matron for female prisoners and for any juveniles. Clara didn't like leaving juveniles in the jail overnight so she took them home and fed them a good, home cooked meal. She had a creative way of making sure none of them escaped. Before they went to bed for the night she had them strip down and then give her all of their clothes, which she put for safe keeping in her own bedroom. Each one then received one of her old nightgowns for the evening. Clara figured, correctly, that teenage boys would not want to escape wearing a woman's nightgown!

Sometimes women prisoners had children whom Clara helped care for. In an effort to help the mothers, she would often hire the women to clean for her. She never carried a gun on her person but kept a Colt 32 revolver under the seat in her vehicle.

While working, Clara Penny was the epitome of a professional officer of the law. When off duty, Clara liked to have fun! She loved to dress to the hilt, and "put on the dog," as she called it. She would go out of town to party, either across the border in California to The Sidewinder Café and Bar. Or she would go over Telegraph Pass to Liguerta. Her favorite companions were her grandsons. They went everywhere with her and they loved it! Sometimes they were called upon to be a canasta partner or a dance partner. On other occasions they had to bar hop with her looking for her youngest son, Billy. Billy would see her coming and would race behind the bar and hide under it. Clara would come in the bar looking for him and with a blank stare the bartender would say, "No, I haven't seen Billy." Her grandchildren remember a hard and fast rule that Clara had regarding holidays- NO ONE eats till everyone is here.

"Puttin' on the dog" with her friends, (Clara center), 1930's.

Clara loved going into the desert for picnics, again her favorite companions were her grandsons. Dave Penny remembers those picnics. "My grandmother was a fun person to be around. She had a colorful vocabulary. She could hold her own on a pier of sailors! She pickled everything including pickled eggs in beet juice making them turn pink, she had pickled okra and always brought along sliced carrots. We had hot dogs that were roasted over a campfire. When we were older, we brought our friends over, whether there were six or sixteen hungry boys, she delighted in whipping up a meal for us. She could do this usually in less than 30 minutes. Her specialty was chicken and dumplings or green tomato pie and peach cobbler. I especially loved her cookie jar; it was always full! When she died, it was what I wanted of hers, the cookie jar."

Without a doubt, Clara's most famous prisoner was Winnie Ruth Judd*. Winnie Ruth Judd was accused of the 1931 Trunk Murders in which she supposedly killed her two best friends, then hacked up their bodies, stuffed them in trunks and shipped them to Los Angeles, California. It was a sensational trial that took America's eyes, at least for a while, off the Great Depression.

Winnie Ruth Judd was finally declared insane and was confined to the Arizona State Hospital in Phoenix. On one of her many escapes, she

Clara (right) pictured transporting Winnie Ruth Judd (center), December 1939.

walked 180 miles to Yuma. While in custody in Yuma, Clara acted as matron and on the long drive back to Phoenix; Clara accompanied the other officers acting as the female matron.

It was during this time that Clara and Winnie became friends. From then on, whenever Clara went to Phoenix she would stop in and see Winnie at the State Hospital and get her hair done. Winnie had started a little hair salon at the hospital. She would do other patients hair for free but soon others from the outside wanted to come to Winnie as she did such an excellent job, and for only .25 cents. On one of these occasions, her grandson accompanied her to the State Hospital. She implored young Dave to come in while she had her hair done and meet Winnie Ruth Judd. "Dave, please come in and meet her. You will really like her. I know she would like to meet you, I have talked about you so much." But Dave could not bring himself to go in. "I was just too frightened." Dave said, decades later. "I regret to this day that I didn't go in and meet her." Finally, a local, rather well to do beautician complained that they were losing business to Winnie Ruth Judd and she was forced to shut down.

Clara's relatives in Ohio had been a little nervous initially about her job as Deputy Sheriff of Yuma County. Her family was HORRIFIED to read about her in a *True Detective Magazine* about the capture of Winnie Ruth Judd. They called her on the phone and begged her to give up this dangerous job.

One day it was Clara's turn to be HORRIFIED to see that a cooler had been confiscated from a high school party that had been broken up over the weekend. On the cooler was the name "Penny." Clara called her grandsons and confronted them. Then she told them, "I don't ever want to see anything in the evidence room again with the name "Penny" on it!"

Clara worked as the Deputy Sheriff of Yuma County until her retirement in 1964. All who knew her respected her. In 1970, Clara Penny died at the age of 73.

*I initially was going to include a short story about Winnie Ruth Judd, based on the things Dave Penny told me his grandmother knew about her. The story grew, and grew, and I became more and more interested. After doing further research, it was out of the question to include the story in this book as it would have overwhelmed it. To learn more about Winnie Ruth Judd, read my short eBook, 25 pages, The 1931 Trunk Murders: The Story of Winnie Ruth Judd. Available at all eBook stores for .99 cents.

Alvin Booth 1868-1937

The baby born in 1868, three years after the Civil War ended to Adam and Lucy Booth in Hillsboro Texas, would have a life much different than his parents. He was born free, not by emancipation, but by birthright. He grew up and became a janitor, errand boy and watchman at the Sturgess National Bank of Hillsboro. His integrity and loyalty were well admired and everyone liked him.

A cashier at the bank, J.N. Porter had accumulated several business interests in Arizona. When Mr. Porter moved to Globe, Arizona, he took Alvin with him as a valet. There was no bank in Globe at the time and Porter organized the First National Bank and Alvin became janitor and body guard to "Mistah Po'ter" as he called him. Alvin was resplendent in the new uniform and cap that Melvin Traylor, President of First National Bank in Chicago had purchased for him. Mr. Traylor knew Alvin from his time in Texas and liked him immensely. He thought it would do the frontier town of Globe good to see such finery every time they went to the bank. He couldn't think of anyone else who would do it more justice than Alvin. Traylor supplied the best of uniforms and caps for Alvin for many years.

Alvin was thrifty and shrewd and was able to save a good deal of money. He invested in a variety of enterprises along with his white friends. He bought up a good amount of rental properties in Globe and became a prosperous landlord with rents derived from his mostly white tenants. In spite of his growing wealth, he continued on with his janitorial duties at the bank.

"Alvin," said Mr. Porter one day, "You have too much idle money lying around. You ought to put it to work." Alvin replied, "Yes, Mistah Po'ter, all the time you have tellin' me: save your money, and don't let nobody fool you into buyin' sometin' you don't know nothin' about. Now you tell me to do it and I don't know nothin' about it, but I always does what YOU tell me."

During the Great Depression, Mr. Porter was nearly wiped out. He fell ill in Los Angeles and when Alvin heard of the distress of his friend, whom he idolized, he hastened to his side. He took all the available cash he could get his hands on, $10,000.00 and handed it over to Mr. Porter upon his arrival as an outright gift. "Mistah. Po'ter, this is all I could get in a hurry, but you can have everything I've got in this world. You are my best friend. You have helped me to get what I got and you showed me how to get more. I can start over and get along, because I learned how from you. What you need is a good rest. When you need more money, you jest let me know. This is a little present from me, you don't tell nobody nothing, you don't owe me nothing. It's me that owes you EVERYTHING." Not long afterward, Mr. Porter died.

Alvin died in 1937, respected by the entire community, and is buried in the white section of the Globe Cemetery. He is truly one of Arizona's Black Pioneers.

EPILOGUE

This story about Alvin Booth came from a volunteer at the Gila County Museum in Globe, Arizona. The volunteer made copies for me of the original stories that had been written about Alvin Booth. Along with this fascinating story was an article showing a revolver, which sold for $69,000. I glanced over the article and looked at the picture of the revolver. It was a nice looking gun, but I couldn't imagine how it could possibly have sold for so much. I asked the volunteer. "Why $69,000?" His simple reply, "Because it belonged to Alvin Booth."

GABRIELLE "DOLLIE" LAYRAL DARDLEY PRESLI TOPP FRETZ MELVIN WILEY (AND A FEW OTHERS) 1890-1962

Dollie was born in France in 1890 and came to the United States as a young teen working as a maid for an Italian family. In 1906, at the tender age of 15, she started her career as a prostitute in the Nevada gold fields. She arrived in Prescott, Arizona in 1909. She "worked" for Leonard Topp who abused her and beat her regularly. One day he asked her to marry him, and the next day he stole all her jewelry and ran off with another woman. Dollie followed him to Los Angeles, California where she tracked him down. She found him at a bar, pulled out a revolver, which had been concealed in a fur muff, and killed him. In a spectacular trial she was acquitted, winning the jury, the media and everyone else's sympathies.

She returned to Prescott and continued in the business she left, but this time in management as a Madam. She married quickly and frequently as her husbands died quickly and frequently.

In 1928, Dollie was looking forward to spending an enjoyable evening at the theatre. A silent movie was being shown at Prescott's Elks Theatre and Dollie was looking forward to seeing it. Much to her surprise she discovered she was the star of the movie! The movie was about the murder of Leonard Topp and not only was it clearly her story, they even used her name. Outraged, she sued the movie producer and the studio, and WON! She added her portion of the $50,000 awarded to her growing bank account. It was this lawsuit that led to the Privacy Act, which we have in place today.

Dollie was often seen on the streets of Prescott but you never would have guessed her occupation. Her hair was always dyed bright red, but never the same red. She dressed in the most elegant and exquisite fashion from head to toe, with an occasional fur to set off the ensemble. But her signature accessories, which she always wore, were her fabulous diamonds. Dollie was dripping in diamonds; diamond necklaces, diamond earrings, diamond bracelets and diamond rings were worn in abundance. It is said she had the largest collection of diamonds in the state of Arizona.

A number of years and a number of husbands later, Dollie married for the last time in 1937. The lucky man was George Wiley from Salome, Arizona. Salome is 100 miles west of Phoenix and desolate now, but extremely desolate then. George met Dollie in Prescott and fell for her in a big way. The description of the marriage is quite comical. Dolly, a 47 year-old madam, complete with her diamonds. George, ex-bootlegger, with a face as red and as round as a tomato. The couple was married by Yavapai County Judge, Gordon Clark, 3 and 1/2 feet tall, known as the "midget judge".

In Salome, George ran a number of small tourist type businesses and Dollie set up her business as well. George died a few years later of "suicide" by rat poison. Rat poison was as much a common theme in Dollie's life as diamonds.

Dollie's best friend, Mae Grisson, also died mysteriously at the same time. Mae was in the hospital recovering from a minor accident, which involved both George Wiley and Dollie. She died mysteriously the day before she was to be released, after a visit from Dollie.

Dollie "retired" after George's death. He had left her enough money to live comfortably. She remained in Salome until her death in 1962 at the age of 72.

Six men were either shot, poisoned or died under mysterious circumstances. There could be more. A number of years in her life are unaccounted for.

GLEN AND BESSIE HYDE

Glen Hyde leaned against a stump and gazed out at the potato fields. He and his father, Rollin, had been working the fields for years since their arrival in Kimberly, Idaho near Twin Falls. Rollin, a widower, had arrived in 1915 with two teenagers and 50 cents in his pocket. It hadn't always been that way. Rollin Hyde was well on his way to becoming a millionaire in the bustling city of Spokane, Washington, when the stock market panic of 1893 hit. The Hyde family lost everything. Although Glen wasn't born yet, he had heard the tales of life when the family was rich. As Glen looked over the fields there was one thing in life he was absolutely sure about. He did not want to be a potato farmer, or any other kind of farmer for that matter.

Glen turned his thoughts away from potatoes to the beautiful girl he had met. Glen had met Bessie Haley while they were both passengers on a steamer from San Francisco to Los Angeles. What a way to travel! It was the thing to do for young people at the time. Two luxury liners, the *Harvard* and the *Yale* were running four trips a week between Los Angeles and San Francisco. There were over 300 staterooms and 25 luxury suites. A beautiful ballroom was on the ship and jazz bands played through the night. There was great food and plenty of it, all included in the price of the ticket. Although it was Prohibition, the luxury ships were out in international waters so alcohol ran freely. It was an 18 hour trip one way. When Glen and Bessie met on the ship, it was love at first sight, for both of them. Upon arrival in Los Angeles, Bessie abandoned her plans in Los Angeles and headed to Idaho with Glen.

The marriage would have happened sooner, but they had to wait for Bessie's divorce to be final from her high school sweetheart, Earl Helmick. It would be easiest to get the divorce in Nevada, so Bessie moved there, rented a room from an older woman for the six weeks of "residency" she would need to obtain the divorce.

Other than Bessie, Glen's passion was river rafting. If he could only make a living at it! It was the 1920's, the age of adventure. Every year some-one was doing something new and daring. In 1927, Charles Lindbergh had flown the *Spirit of St. Louis* across the ocean and achieved worldwide fame. Amelia Earhart was going to be the first woman to cross the Atlantic. She would become famous too. People who were completely unknown one day were front page news the next. If Glen could do something that no one else had done- be the first, the fastest, break a record- it could lead to all kinds of possibilities; a book contract, speaking engagements and the biggest plum of all, to be included in the vaudeville lecture circuit.

After their marriage on April 12, 1928, a day after the divorce was granted, Glen and Bessie began to formulate a plan. A fuzzy dream at first, it began to take shape. They would plan a "Honeymoon Trip," river rafting the Colorado River. Glen was an experienced river runner, having run the Snake, Salmon and the Peace River in Canada. Bessie had never done any type of river running. It would be an adventurous trip. Fun was not the object or purpose of the trip. Making money was the end goal. Glen had FOUR "firsts" in mind. They would break a SPEED RECORD through the Grand Canyon. Although a total of 45 men had gone through the canyon by 1928, no woman had ever run the river. Bessie, all ninety pounds of her, would be the FIRST WOMAN. They would run ALL the rapids in the Canyon. Some before them had "lined" their boats

Glen and Bessie, mid-November 1928, taken by Emery Kolb at his studio on the Grand Canyon rim.

around difficult rapids and had not run them. The icing on the cake: they would do it all WITHOUT LIFE PRESERVERS.

All that spring and summer the Hyde's eagerly planned their trip. They read everything they could find about the river, the terrain and the rapids. Both Glen and Bessie were very bright, both had done public speaking, and some acting. They both could write. Bessie could also draw. They imagined the book before they even set foot on the river, both of them writing and Bessie doing the illustrations. They would take a camera along, and many rolls of film.

After the harvest was complete, they set out for Green River, Utah where they would begin. With $50.00 and two days, Glen built the boat himself using lumber he purchased in Green River. It was a type of boat he had used on previous trips called a "sweep scow." It was 20 feet long, 5 feet wide and three feet deep. Harry Howland, a Green River local's appraisal of the boat, "It looks like a floating coffin."

They set out on October 20, 1928. The trip from Green River to Lee's Ferry was for the most part pleasant and uneventful. The fall weather was warm and days were pleasant. The scenery was beautiful and they saw an abundance of wildlife. The food they had brought along tasted wonderful. The scow was nicknamed, *Rain-in-the-Face*. When they arrived at Lee's Ferry, the Johnson brothers, who were running the Ferry, implored them to go no further. And as everyone they met would do, the brothers begged

Rowing their scow in Marble Canyon, early November 1928, heading out from Lee's Ferry.

Glen and Bessie to take life preservers. Glen and Bessie refused, and headed past the "point of no return" down the 60 miles of Marble Canyon.

Here the walls of the Canyon were steep; every day was getting shorter, and colder. The sun was moving further and further into the southern sky. Some days, the sun never reached the Canyon floor. The lovely fall they had experienced was now approaching winter. The beautiful weather they experienced in Utah was over. Two back-to-back storms, one with terrible wind and the other with drenching rain hit them. At times they noticed ice forming along the bank of the river and near the rock outcroppings.

When they hit Sockdolager Rapid it sent Glen overboard out of the boat. Terrified, Bessie threw Glen a rope and managed to pull him aboard. They were both badly shaken. The next day, they hit Grapevine Rapid, just as frightening as Sockdolager. They were re-

One of the last photos taken of the couple on the Colorado River in late November.

lieved to finally get to Bright Angel Creek. Here the new Kaibab Trail had been completed. After a quick lunch, Glen and Bessie headed up the trail to the rim of the Grand Canyon. The hike, 7 miles almost straight up, gaining 5,000 feet in elevation, was beautiful with views changing every minute with the changing light. Clouds formed and for a brief time they walked in a snowstorm. Bessie described it as "beautiful." However, once they reached the top they were dismayed that the Kaibab Trail came out at Yaki Point, 6 miles from Grand Canyon Village. It was getting dark, and they had no option but to start walking. After 3 miles, a car came along and picked them up.

They spent three days at the rim. Unable to afford the beautiful El Tovar Hotel, they rented a cabin, which after nearly a month on the boat, seemed like heaven. A reporter was there from the *Denver Post* and interviewed them, focusing primarily on Bessie and quoting her at length. Glen had been right! The feminine angle was already paying off. The interview was picked up by the Associated Press and carried in newspapers across the country. Their first step on their road to fame! Emery Kolb took their pictures, drove them around the Canyon, and invited them to his lecture. As the Johnson brothers had done at Lee's Ferry, Emery Kolb begged them to take life preservers. Kolb offered to give them some of his own. When they refused, Kolb suggested inner tubes, better than nothing, he thought.

The last photo taken of the couple by Adolph Sutro at Hermit's Rest Camp.

After resupplying, they headed back down to resume their trip. They had traveled 375 miles and had 430 more to go. They left Grand Canyon Village on the morning of November 17. One of the last people to see Glen and Bessie was Adolph Sutro. A wealthy tourist he was looking for a bit of adventure. He rode on their scow for 8 miles to Hermit's Rest Camp and was not disappointed! His description of the young couple is extremely important as there was so much controversy and conflicting information from those who remember them while they were on the rim. His description, 30 years later:

> *She was very petite, I was scared in the rapid, the girl was terrified, she registered stark fear. I was skeptical of their outfit; it was the most inadequately equipped outfit I had ever seen. I couldn't understand how they got to Bright Angel. We had quite a few conversations; they made the trip hoping they could get theatrical showing. Emphasis was on money that would be made in show business. Obvious the whole object of the trip was to make money. The feminine angle is always important. He (Glen) was decent—not domineering—irresponsible. I waved them good-bye and*

climbed out on a mule.

Sutro had signed on for one of the most difficult runs through the Canyon. He goes on with his quite humorous philosophy on life:

My unfailing guiding light in life has been the precept that it is better to be a live coward than a dead hero. This has permitted me to avoid many perils such as wing walking on aeroplanes, running for political office or committing matrimony. So in accordance with the foregoing, may I point out with pride, that I disembarked permanently at the very first possible landing spot. A rather comprehensive experience in sailing small boats in the North Pacific assisted me in formulating my judgement.

After Sutro's departure, Glen and Bessie would be facing some of the most perilous rapids. The worst was yet to come. That wasn't all, Bessie was most likely pregnant. From people who talked to them, from her notes in her journal, this seems a very likely possibility.

When Glen and Bessie Hyde failed to arrive at Needles, California on December 9, 1928, Glen's 30th birthday, Glen's father, Rollin Hyde became alarmed. On December 12th, when still no word came, he boarded a train for Las Vegas, Nevada. He made a heroic attempt to find his only son and daughter-in-law.

Adolph Sutro got the adventure he was looking for by rafting 8 harrowing miles with the Hydes.

He contacted everyone he knew; pulled every political favor he could, and spent every penny he had to find them. A plane enlisted in the search was first to spot the scow. It was eerily sitting empty in a quiet pool of water. Since it was intact, there was hope the young couple would be found. The planes scoured the river, looking for signs of life, but nothing. When Kolb, who had signed on to the search found several places the Hyde's had camped, landings they had made, and marks they carved on the boat as each day passed, it all points to November 30th as the day the scow and its occupants parted company. The scow was found fully intact. All their clothing was aboard, an abundance of food, the camera, Glen's rifle, Bessie's journal, the only thing that was missing was Bessie's sketchbook.

EPILOGUE

What happened to Glen and Bessie Hyde? The answer is we will never know for sure. The bodies were never found. Had pieces of the boat been found, the easy assumption would be they crashed and drowned in the river. Because the boat was found, completely loaded and completely intact, floating in a quiet pool, mystery has surrounded it for decades. There are as many theories as there are people who have run the Colorado or have read about Glen and Bessie.

I have found this story to be one of the most interesting and intriguing stories I have ever written about. I hope to do further research and write a short eBook, focusing exclusively on this story. I highly recommend Brad Dimock's excellent book, Sunk Without a Sound, 2001, by Fretwater Press.

Fred Kabotie

It seemed wherever I went in Flagstaff I saw him. He often rode the same city bus I did. I turned the corner downtown one day and there he was. I looked up from the desk at the public library and he was sitting across from me. One winter morning, I was standing in line at 5 a.m. to board an Amtrak train and I turned around and he was in line behind me. I blurted out, "One of us is a stalker!" We both burst out laughing.

After boarding the train I usually abandon my coach seat as quickly as possible and head to the observation car. There I sit for most of the day, enjoying the scenery and visiting with the other Amtrak passengers. Not long after I arrived in the observation car and sat down, my "friend" arrived as well and we sat and visited until he got off in Gallup, New Mexico. His name is Ed Kabotie. He is the great-grandson of the famous Hopi artist, Fred Kabotie. He was often at the museum, where he got off and on the city bus, because he was an Artist in Residence at the Museum of Northern Arizona. I discovered I knew his sister, Meg, because she was running the

One of the murals Fred painted at the Grand Canyon Watchtower,
Photo courtesy Julie McDonald.

Museum of Northern Arizona Bookstore where I sold my books and a line of postcards. He was downtown frequently where he often played music.

That day he was riding the train to visit relatives. He told me the fascinating story of his great grandparents, Fred and Alice Kabotie. Fred was born in Shungopavi, Second Mesa around 1900 on the Hopi Reservation. Both he and Alice were forced to attend government boarding schools far from home. They met at Phoenix Indian School when

Fred explaining the Snake Legend mural, 1932.

Fred delivered a package to her from her brother. Ed said, "When it came time for their own children to go to boarding school, they refused. The government put all kinds of pressure on them, but they resisted." Ed went on. "My great grandfather was a self-taught artist. He painted scenes from our culture which reflected Hopi life and told a story. He was commissioned by Mary Jane Colter to paint the murals at the Watchtower at Grand Canyon National Park in 1933." I enjoyed visiting with Ed Kabotie on the train and I could hardly wait to learn more about his famous great grandfather.

Not long afterwards I visited Petrified Forest National Park and stopped at the Painted Desert Inn, which is a historic inn within the park. Much to my surprise, Fred Kabotie had painted the beautiful murals there in May and June of 1948. In 1937, Fred Kabotie began teaching art at the new Hopi High School where he taught for 22 years. He painted over 500 paintings during his life time and taught art to hundreds of Hopi students. It was a lifelong passion to encourage native artists and craftsman.

Fred pictured with Eleanor Roosevelt, 1941, at the Indian Art of the United States exhibition.

He advised and painted murals at the Museum of Modern Art in 1941 while constantly advocating for Indian artistry. He was one of the founders of the world famous Hopi Cultural Center. He was internationally known and left a great legacy through his own art work and that of his students. He received the prestigious John Simon Guggenheim Memorial Fellowship in 1945. He remarks when remembering the $2,000 stipend he received from the award, "If it had been two million, Alice and I could not have been more pleased and grateful."

The Museum of Northern Arizona in Flagstaff encouraged Kabotie and his cousin Paul Saufkie to develop a jewelry style unique to Hopis. They created designs inspired by Hopi pottery. Fred Kabotie's first piece of jewelry was commissioned as a gift to Eleanor Roosevelt. After World War II, with funding from the GI Bill, Fred and his cousin taught returning Hopi veterans the art of silversmith, with Kabotie teaching design and Saufkie teaching technique. To showcase their students work, they created the Hopi Silvercraft Cooperative Guild in 1949.

As he grew older, he found his greatest pleasure was spending time with his grandchildren and working his fields, participating in Hopi life and culture. He tells a humorous story when he is in his late 70's in the autobiography about his life, Fred Kabotie: Hopi Indian Artist. "In my office over at the craft guild I have a big appointment calendar. Somehow each year it gets busier- Tiffany Foundation meetings in New York, my teaching in California, judging exhibits at the Gallup-Intertribal Ceremonial, Hopi Cultural Center board meetings, Tribal Council meetings.

'We'd like to have you on our board,' the directors of the Hopi Center for Human Services said a year or so ago. "I can't." I told them. "You fellows call meetings at 7:30, and I am still out in my cornfield; I rather stay out in my field and work."

Fred and Alice had three children, their oldest Freddie, drowned in a tragic accident at the age of 14. Their second son, Michael, also became a famous Hopi artist. Their daughter, Hattie, taught kindergarten in Riverside, California, while husband Dwight taught Native American Studies at a local college. Dwight and Hattie had three children.

Fred Kabotie died in 1986.

When talking to my friend David, an art expert, about this story he told me he had been asked to value the murals Fred Kabotie painted at the Watchtower for insurance purposes. Curiosity got the best of me and I asked him, "What did you value them at?" He replied, "Easily in the millions, but quite frankly, they are priceless."

CHARLIE ALLEN

For those of us who love Oak Creek Canyon we owe a debt of gratitude to a man most of us have never heard of. Charlie Allen worked for the railroad as a surveyor. At some point he had an accident and was disabled. One of his favorite places was Oak Creek Canyon. He began coming in the early 1900's and into the 1930's. He came every summer between 1912 and 1923. In addition to being a surveyor he was a professional photographer. Photography equipment was rare at that time and certainly none of the homesteaders in the canyon had access to photography.

Because of Charlie Allen we have hundreds of high quality photographs of individuals, families, cabins and homesteads as well as school groups, animals and picnics that contributed to the priceless heritage of Oak Creek Canyon. Allen's Bend Trail near Junipine Resort is named for him.

Jess Purtymun playing his accordion. The inscription on the cave wall reads, "Our Cave kitchen, 1912, Oak Canyon. Photo courtesy of Sedona Heritage Museum.

Purtymun family with Bear Howard standing far right. Courtesy of the Sedona Heritage Museum.

Amanda "Judge" Miller 1878-1966

I LOVE cemeteries! One of my favorite things to do is visit old pioneer cemeteries. When my kids were growing up they would just groan whenever we passed one. When they got older, and were usually doing the driving they would say, "10 minutes Mom, you've got 10 minutes."

The great thing about the local Citizens Cemetery in Flagstaff, Arizona is that I can go there whenever I want, for as long as I want. Plus I have lots of friends and family there. One day in 2012, I was wandering around in the cemetery when I came upon a grave I had never seen before, "Wow, I thought, that looks so interesting." The stone read, "Amanda "Judge" Miller, born of slaves, A Flagstaff Pioneer." I was relatively confident I could find out about it so I began asking around. None of my friends had ever heard of Amanda "Judge" Miller. Was she really a Judge? I checked at the cemetery office. They couldn't tell me anything, nor did they know who had placed the grave marker there. I looked for information at the library- zip! I went to the Pioneer Museum. No, they didn't know anything either. Vincent Ritchie worked at Pioneer Museum and although he wasn't from Flagstaff, he was an expert in Arizona Black History and is black himself. He couldn't find anything. Now I was completely frustrated. The only shred of evidence I had found was a 1929 phone book that listed Amanda Miller as living on Terrace Avenue. That seemed a bit odd as someone I was interviewing for another story had just mentioned to me that blacks were not allowed to purchase property north of the railroad tracks until after World War ll.

This was the first story that had defeated me. If I couldn't write about Amanda, I decided to write about another freed slave, one I had heard about while in Ouray, Colorado. The wonderful story of Clara Brown, the first story in "Unbreakable Dolls, Too" is one of my favorites and easily in the top three favorite stories of my readers.

In the summer of 2014, I was again at the Pioneer Museum in Flagstaff doing research for yet another story. Vince was there that day and said, "Hi, Julie! I think you will find this very interesting." He handed me some papers he had been working on. I felt like I was in the pioneer history twilight zone. Here was all sorts of information about Amanda "Judge" Miller. "Vince", I said, "this is the story I was trying to find a couple of years ago. "Oh my goodness!" Vince exclaimed, "It was YOU! I couldn't remember who had told me about the grave at the cemetery."

After I left that day in 2012, Vince kept thinking about the cemetery gravestone and finally went to the cemetery to see it for himself. He and his family have been working very hard to put together a family genealogy. For anyone with a history of slavery, this is extremely difficult. Births and deaths were not recorded, slaves didn't have last names and after the Emancipation Proclamation they either took the name of their former owners or made up a new name for themselves.

As it turns out, incredibly, Amanda Miller is one of Vincent Ritchie's relatives, a missing piece they had been trying to track down and were so excited to finally find it! In finding Amanda, they found an entire family line complete with history and biography of some of the family members.

Amanda was light enough to "pass" in other words, if you didn't know of her slave heritage, you would not have guessed. She was from Toccoa, Georgia. She left Georgia sometime in the 1890's and traveled west. She most likely traveled by foot for all or most of the way; it would have taken her at least 2 years. She would have stopped from time to time to work for people until she enough money to travel on. She arrived in Flagstaff, Arizona and went to work as a housekeeper. This was her occupation her entire life. She apparently made enough to eventually purchase her own home on Terrace Street, a pleasant neighborhood which overlooks Route 66. Her house is still there. The "Judge" was her father's name and that is why it appears as her middle name. She was one of 10 children. One of the family's find was an interview with her mother at the age of 100 in 1937. The interviewer describes Harriet Miller this way:

Aunt Harriet Miller, a chipper and spry Indian half-breed, thinks she is about 100 years old. It is remarkable that one so old should possess so much energy and animation. She is tall and spare, with a wrinkled face, bright eyes, a kindly expression, and she wears her iron grey hair wound in a knob in the manner of a past generation. Aunt Harriet was neatly dressed as she had just returned from a trip to Cornelia to see some of her folks. She did not appear at all tired from the trip and seemed glad to discuss the old days.

"My father," said Aunt Harriet "was a Cherokee Indian named Green Norris, and my mother was a white woman named Betsey Richards. You see, I am mixed. My mother give me to Mr. George Naves when I was three years old. He lived in de mountains of South Carolina, jest across de river. He didn't own his home. He was an overseer for de Jarrett's, old man Kennedy Jarrett. Honey, people was just like dey is now, some good, some bad. Mr. Naves was a good man. Dese here Jarrett's were good to deir slaves. Some of the white ladies taught deir slaves, yes'm, some of 'em did. Slaves had a half a day off on Saturday, Dey had frolics at night, quilting's, dances, corn shuckings, and played de fiddle. Dey stays in their quarters on Sunday or go to church. Dey go to the same church wid de whitefoks."

The interview continues on for about four pages where she names all of her 10 children, and mentions that Judge, her husband died in 1900. She says she has 40 grandchildren but, "last time I was counting the great-grandchildren, I could count 'em up to 37 but some have come in since den."

She closes the interview by saying, "Dis old lady been swinging on a limb a long time and she going to swing off from here some time. I'm near 100 and I won't be here long, but when I go, I wants to go in peace wid everybody."

There was much truth in that gravestone: Amanda "Judge" Miller, Born of Slaves, a Flagstaff Pioneer.

HADJI ALI (HI JOLLY) 1838-1902

WANTED: Men of Middle Eastern descent, familiar with the care, feeding and driving of camels. Free, all expense trip to the United States of America!

Between 1848 and 1854 The United States added a huge amount of real estate thanks to the Mexican American War and the Gadsden Purchase. No one was quite sure exactly what we had obtained but the prevailing assumption was a vast desert. Plans were made to build military forts all across this new land but how could the forts be stocked with provisions? George Crosman thought the transportation answer was camels.

Camels were relatively easy to obtain, camel drovers were not. Among the best of them was Hadji Ali. His name was difficult to pronounce and therefore it was reduced to Hi Jolly. If there ever was a "camel whisperer" it would have been Hi Jolly. As one observer described: "There was only one man who appeared to have any influence over the bewildered beasts. Slender build and in his middle 30's, the assembled Texans saw him as a rather attractive chap, with a flashing, white-toothed smile, black eyes and curly hair. Moving quietly among the restless animals, he spoke to them in a soft, foreign tongue, reassuring them, placating then, as a mother might speak to a fretful child. Gradually it became apparent to the crowd that this dark-skinned fellow alone, was bringing order out of chaos."

Edward Beale (Beale Wagon Road), was in charge of the camel experiment. Beale joined the camel troop in Albuquerque, New Mexico and immediately realized camel drovers, alcohol and bordellos do not make a pretty combination, so from then on, they took the rural route.

They passed through the Painted Desert and across the base of the San Francisco Peaks near what eventually would become Flagstaff, Arizona. The Beale Wagon Road actually is less than 1/4 mile from my house and I often walk on a well-marked "Beale Wagon Road" trail not far from home as it heads west. The road then passed near the South Rim of the Grand Canyon and then on to Peach Springs and Kingman. Beale effectively laid the groundwork for what would become first a well-used wagon train road. It eventually would be part of Route 66, then Interstate 40. The real test for the camels, which had performed magnificently up to this point, would be the Colorado River. Would the camels cross? With Sa'id, Hi Jolly's favorite camel in the lead, and Hi Jolly whispering sweet nothings into the camel's ear all the camels crossed safely to the other side. Two horses, 10 mules and a large number of sheep drowned while trying to cross. The date was October 17, 1857.

The camel experiment was a huge success! We would be seeing camels all across the southwest had fate not intervened. 1) Edward Beale's enthusiasm for camels did not transfer to the military brass in Washington. 2) The nation was on the verge of the Civil War. No one cared about camels, or anything else, in the desert southwest.

The camels were decommissioned and Hi Jolly was out of a job. The camels were sold to zoos, plantations, and mines. Many camels either escaped or became feral and Hi Jolly spent a lifetime rounding them up again. He kept a sizeable herd and using the camels to carry heavy loads, he established a transportation route from Yuma to Gila Bend and then over to Tucson, and back again.

Their wedding photo taken after he became a citizen, 1880.

While in Tucson he met a Sonoran woman, Gertrudis Serna whom he married in 1880. Together they had two daughters, Amelia and Herminia. He found Tucson, and marriage, too confining and soon he was out in the desert again. He rounded up more feral camels near present day Quartzsite and became somewhat of a celebrity there.

A wild breeding population of about 100 adult camels was also located over 100 miles away in the Gila River Valley. They adapted to cacti and mesquite. They were not only surviving, but thriving, showing good vigor, and high reproductive rates.

Hi Jolly died in 1902 at the age of 64. He died on a lonely road while "out looking for camels." The last camel from the original herd died at the Los Angeles Zoo at the age of 80. Its ashes were put in a vault with the stone pyramid at Hi Jolly's last camp near Quartzsite. The last feral camel was captured in 1946.

Epilogue

Quartzsite celebrates an annual festival called Hi Jolly Daze. Quartzsite has been home to the Hi Jolly Rock Shop, The Hi Ali Motel and Hi Jolly Liquors. The Ballad of Hi Jolly has been sung around many a western camp fire.

A number of years ago, an Arizona historian who is a stickler for accuracy was annoyed by the sign along Interstate 40 near Seligman, for Hi Jolly Road. She wrote to the Arizona Department of Transportation asking that the sign be changed to Hadji Ali since that was his real name and no one, including ADOT, should be using his American nick-name. A few months later she drove by the sign, and saw that ADOT had indeed changed the sign at her request. It now reads Jolly Road.

In 1935, Arizona Governor Benjamin Mauer dedicated a memorial to Hi Jolly at the Quartzsite Cemetery. It is one of the most popular visited sites in the area.

CLYDE TOMBAUGH 1906-1997

As the bumper sticker says, "If I had known how much fun grand-children were, I would have had them first." That is how I feel about my 6 grandchildren! I LOVE doing things with them. Four of them moved to Albuquerque a couple of years ago. I was already plotting how I could "snatch" them on the train. Since my son is a pastor, he obviously can't take off the week of Easter. Lucky for me, their last spring break was the week of Easter, so I had them for a whole week! We had SO much fun! We went to the Aquaplex, Walnut Canyon, ice skating, on picnics, to the library and parks. One of the 8 year old twins, Jason really loves space. I thought I would take them to Lowell Observatory. Jason would love it! Trenton, Davis and I would have to endure it for Jason's sake. It was mar-velous! We spent almost the whole day there going to different programs and events and, looking through telescopes.

One of the presenters told the story of how Pluto had been discovered by Clyde Tombaugh, a "space observer" who was also working as a cus-

todian at the observatory. I had been raised in Flagstaff, Clyde Tombaugh, who was he? I had never heard of him before. Where was I when they taught that in school? Not paying attention? That is a distinct possibility.

As soon as I returned the three boys to their parents and little sister, Kara, I was at the library looking for information. Clyde Tombaugh was a farm boy from the mid-west. When he was 12 years old his Uncle Lee arrived at his house and set up a telescope in the back yard. Clyde had never looked through a telescope before and he was

Clyde with the telescope he discovered Pluto with, in 1931.

fascinated. Long after everyone else had enough, Clyde and Uncle Lee looked through the telescope and talked about the moon and stars. Uncle Lee loaned Clyde a book on astronomy and Clyde read it through so many times he almost had it memorized.

When Clyde was sixteen his family moved to Kansas from Illinois. There he continued at high school and helped on the farm. He really wanted to go to college to become an astronomer, but there wasn't enough money. He couldn't afford to purchase telescopes, so he made his own. One summer, three years after high school graduation, the oats and wheat were doing so well, it would be a bumper crop. Clyde knew that with the money from the harvest now he could go to college. Then devastation hit. A hail storm wiped out the entire crop. There would be no money for school. Clyde decided no matter what, he would try to work in the field of astronomy. He sent his best drawings of Jupiter and Mars to Lowell Observatory in Flagstaff, Arizona. Clyde was overjoyed when they offered him a job! He came to Flagstaff in January of 1929. He hoped it would work out, as he didn't have enough money for a train ticket back to Kansas. He could work with the telescope and new camera, but the astronomers at Lowell Observatory needed other work done as well. Sidewalks and the telescope roof needed to be cleared of snow. Flagstaff gets an average of 100 inches of snow every year! He would give visitors guided tours. He could work at night as much as he liked. Night after night he took pictures of the sky, day after day he did his custodial jobs and looked over the pictures of the sky he had taken the night before.

For 25 years, the astronomers at Lowell, and other observatories had been searching for the elusive Planet X. They had never been able to find it. For a few months the astronomers looked at the photos Clyde was taking, but eventually they weren't looking at them anymore. They told Clyde he could do both jobs, taking the photos, and looking through them. Of course he continued on with his custodial duties as well. Clyde was a hard worker and determined. He methodically looked with great care through every photo. In February of 1930, 13 months after his arrival in Flagstaff, Clyde Tombaugh found the planet! It took several days to confirm it, but it was true!

Tombaugh was finally able to go to college, graduating from the University in Kansas in 1936. He received his masters in 1939 from the University of Kansas. During World War 11 he was called into active duty and taught celestial navigation. After the war he went on to develop systems for tracking rockets at White Sands, New Mexico. He discovered numerous asteroids, naming them after his wife, Patsy, children, Annette and Alden, his grandchildren and other family members. He also went on to discover the hundreds of starts, star clusters and star galaxies.

After reading several articles and going through books about Clyde Tombaugh I realized I HAD been paying attention in school. The discovery of Pluto was not really credited to Clyde Tombaugh, the farm boy from Kansas with only a high school education, until recently. Other men, more "important" astronomers who had been working for decades to find the ninth planet took the credit for themselves. Only in Kansas was Tombaugh adequately recognized.

Clyde Tombaugh died in Las Cruces, New Mexico in 1996 at the age of ninety. He was recognized and respected the world over for all of his accomplishments in the field of Astronomy.

Jennie Bauter

Jennie Bauter arrived in Jerome during its mining heyday in the 1890's. When she was born and where she came from no one really knows for sure. She came to Jerome to take advantage of the mines and the men that she knew would enjoy the business she intended to set up. Since Jerome was known to burn down on a regular basis, Jennie was pro-active in securing the safety of the lovely building she built upon her arrival. It was WHEN there was a fire, not IF there was a fire.

She went to the fire station and asked to speak to the chief. She made him this proposal, "The next time we have a fire, if you save my building from burning down, I will give you and all the fire fighters free passes to my establishment."

When the next fire happened, the entire block burned down, but Jennie's business was left unscathed. Saved by the heroic fireman and the many volunteers who rushed to help.

Jennie was good to her girls and every Sunday she took all of them to a Sunday dinner at one of Jerome's nicest restaurants. The girls all dressed in their finest attire and spent a relaxing day, enjoying a long leisurely meal. Sundays were slow anyway. Jennie liked to treat the girls to a special day out, and she also thought it was good advertising. Jennie was a successful businesswoman and at one time was considered the richest woman in Arizona.

In 1903 she set her sights on a new boomtown, Acne,

Jennie is pictured on the second floor (center) with her girls at a Jerome brothel.

(now called Goldfield) near the Arizona/Nevada border. Her gambling suitor followed her there. One night Clement Leigh needed money for a bad debt. He went to Jennie's place and insisted that she give him the money. Jennie refused, and terrified, ran out of the building. Clement chased her and shot her several times, hitting her in the back and paralyzing her. As she lay motionless, but conscious, on the street he came up to her and shot her in the head. He then turned the gun on himself and fired into his chest. Although seriously injured, he didn't die. He was tried by a jury and hung in 1907.

EPILOGUE

Everyone who had known Jennie loved her and mourned her death. Both she and Clement were buried in the Pioneer Cemetery in Kingman, Arizona, which was in existence from 1907 to 1917. In 1917 Mohave County began moving the graves to the new Mountain View Cemetery. Mohave County wasn't paying for the moves. The families had to pay for their departed loved ones last excursion. Those who had no families or friends to pay for them were left behind. Years later, Mohave County donated the Pioneer Cemetery property to the school board to build a new school. When children playing on the football field started digging up bones from the graves that were never moved, Mohave authorities sprang into action. The existing graves were exhumed and placed in a solitary grave with a plaque. Both Jennie and Clement are buried together in the end zone of White Cliff Middle School in Kingman, Arizona.

HERMANN WOLF

Hermann Wolf needed to get out of Germany and needed to get out fast. He was wanted for a serious crime that would put him away for life. He did not want to bring shame to his family. Too many Germans were in America, he would be found even there. He had heard about a remote place in the Arizona Territory. Only Navajo Indians lived there. It didn't sound appealing, but it did sound safe.

Hermann Wolf managed to find one of the most remote places in all of the Navajo Reservation, near Grand Falls on the Little Colorado River. There he built a trading post. He welcomed Navajos, Hopis and other friendly tribes. He welcomed Mexicans as well. He wanted nothing to do with any person of Anglo descent. An Anglo person could be a German, a friend of a German or know a German. They could spell his downfall. He was mean to all Anglos, he didn't like them. They in turn, didn't like him either.

Jerry Snow examines a wall still standing at Wolf Post. The wall is double sided and mortar made with mud is between the two walls.

From the beginning, the Navajos called him "Hosteen Chi," Mr. Beaver, the name they had given him during his beaver trapping days.

His goods had to come all the way from Albuquerque, his Indian products and furs taken there by Mexicans and Indian guides who were always amazed to find him alive upon their return. During his first decade his post was attacked time and time again by Paiutes to the west, Apaches from the south, outlaws from every direction. The post was attacked regularly, two to three times a year. It was his Navajo friends that provided protection and without their help, Wolf Post would have been destroyed.

Wolf Post prospered. Wolf was buying imported Rhine Wine from Germany and having it shipped all the way to Arizona. Word spread that Wolf did not use a bank for his money. A legend began that he had a cache of gold. More than once his post was attacked by outlaws looking for the gold that supposedly was hidden in the walls, the floors, or the cracks in the bluffs. The legend persists to this day, but nothing has ever been found.

Shortly after his arrival many others began to come west, travelers, settlers, stockmen and explorers. This meant many new customers who came to Wolf Post on the Little Colorado, not far from Fred Volz Trading Post at Canyon Diablo.

After years of living and trading on the reservation he received word that his brother, Franz, would be coming to visit him from Germany. What an incredible surprise! He had not seen family since he left.

In late August of 1899, Wolf then nearing 80 came to Flagstaff to meet his brother who would be arriving on the train. Three days passed and still his brother did not come. Several days earlier Hermann had begun to feel ill. People in Flagstaff noticed he did not look well. After waiting and waiting, and still his brother did not come, Hermann made the long trip back to his post. He had so wanted to have this special visit with his

Grand Falls on the Little Colorado River.

brother. He reached the post almost helpless and his clerk sent a message to Dr. Miller in Flagstaff, "Come quickly, Wolf is dying!" Dr. Miller came in his buggy, along with Franz Wolf who had just arrived on the train, a distance of about 40 miles, but

Hermann Wolf was dead.

The next day he was buried with his brother doing the funeral oration in the rites of the German Lutheran Church. His brother purchased a beautiful granite tombstone that remains there today. Hermann Wolf is the only man buried at the boot hill near Canyon Diablo that did not die a violent death. The only other grave that can be identified is that of John Shaw.

Damacia Torres Baca 1857-1934

Many a young man left the comforts of home and family in the East or Midwest for the adventurous life of a cowboy. But it wasn't as glamorous as they had anticipated and the thrill quickly wore off. Many a young cowboy found at the Baca Ranch near Heber, Arizona what they were missing from home.

Juan and Damacia had established their small farm and ranch near the wagon trail which connected Pleasant Valley and Holbrook. Many early settlers used this wagon road. Stockmen used the wagon road to drive their sheep and cattle. Juan died in 1903 leaving Damacia, 44 with 7 daughters and one son to raise. Everyone was welcome at the Baca Ranch! When Damacia saw a stranger she would run outside and call out to them, "Come in and have a bite before you travel on." Everyone loved to partake of her generous hospitality. Her kindness extended to all but she particularly had a soft spot for the young cowboys far from home. They loved the home cooked meals and the motherly, kind encouragement of Mrs. Baca. She listened to each of the young cowboys, fed them, cared for them, counseled them and hugged them.

When Damacia Baca died at age 77 in 1934, 200 cowboys were at her funeral, most of them weeping unashamedly.

Helen "Duett" Hunt 1867-1931

Duett looked through her assortment of party dresses hanging in her closet. She picked a pretty pink one, found a hat to match it, and selected a petticoat and white gloves and her best shoes. She carefully placed all of them in her trunk which would be carried in the chuck wagon.

Duett then got dressed for her "job." Duett was her father, Jesse Ellison's, "number one cowboy." She had been tapped to drive cattle to market in Winslow, 75 miles away. Duett was already thinking ahead. After the week long cattle drive, Duett would sell the cattle, which would be loaded in cattle cars, collect the cash and get cleaned up. There would be a dance on Saturday night. No matter how tired Duett was from driving cattle during the day or sleeping on the hard ground at night, she planned on dancing all night long.

Her work clothes consisted of a heavy coarse skirt, a long sleeved shirt, leather jacket, heavy leather boots and leather gloves; a kerchief to wear around her neck and pull up when needed over her mouth to protect her lungs from dust, and of course, a cowboy hat. Other ranch hands would be going with her, but Duett was in charge.

The Ellison family consisted of father Jesse, mother Susan, and 8 children. The oldest son was Pearl, then the six girls, Duett, Lena, Rose, Minnie, Sarah, Mattie and Jesse. With only two sons, Jesse taught all his daughters all aspects of cattle ranching. They learned to ride horses, rope cows, doctor sick animals and shoot both rifle and pistol. The only one exempt was Lena who was frail and nearly blind. She stayed indoors helping her mother, Susan.

Duett with a bear she hunted and shot, 1899.

When the girls weren't working with their father, they were expected to be in the house helping their mother in the kitchen baking or serving. At other times they helped Susan with all the other household chores such as cleaning, washing, ironing, sewing and mending clothes.

All the girls learned to provide southern hospitality to their many guests. It is estimated that 4,000 (FOUR THOUSAND!) people came to the Q Ranch EVERY year! After serving their guests a fine meal, usually with pork as the main dish, Jesse would pull out his fiddle and any one of the girls would join him on the piano. Then the dancing would begin!

Duett cleaned up nicely in one of her many dresses, circa 1890's.

In a September 29, 1901 edition of the San Francisco Call the article stated:

> The Ellison family are royal entertainers of the Southern type and the Ellison dances are famous all over central Arizona. Every unmarried cowboy within a radius of fifty miles of the Ellison Ranch, has at sometime within the last three years, been a suitor of the Ellison girls.

The Ellison family had arrived in beautiful Pleasant Valley just in time for the Pleasant Valley War. The Pleasant Valley War was the most deadly family feud in United States History. As many as 30 men died in the fighting between the Tewksburys and the Grahams. No one was neutral in the feud and the Ellisons joined forces with the Tewksburys. There were also ongoing skirmishes with the Apaches. Duett was far more capable of negotiating with them than her hot tempered father.

George Hunt, an up and coming politician first met Duett in 1890 when he was running for County Recorder of Gila County. He had made a vow to visit every single family in Gila County, which he did. He visited the Ellison family several times and his interest was increasingly on Duett. George Hunt was 28 years old at that time, and Duett was 20.

George W.P. Hunt, first governor of Arizona, served seven terms.

The courtship lasted 16 years. It was mostly through letters. Both parties kept the letters which are of great historical and romantic interest. The letters are infrequent and surprisingly short.

During the 16 year courtship, George had proposed to Duett twice. It seemed that with each proposal an emergency "ranch crises" arose and Duett never felt free to leave. Rumors abounded that her father didn't want to lose his number one cowboy and tried to keep Duett on the ranch.

George tired of all the postponements and sent Duett a telegram with an ultimatum. "If she wanted to be married, she was to be at the home of their friends in Holbrook on February 24, 1904 so they could be married." George must have felt fairly secure she would be there as he sent invitations to their friends as well. Duett arrived with her father Jesse, who gave her away. George was 44 and Duett was 36. They took a long honeymoon trip to Mexico and returned in time for the St. Louis World's Fair. They returned home to Globe via New Orleans.

During their 27 year marriage, which they both considered a happy one, Duett stood by George as he first became Mayor of Globe, served in the Territorial Legislature and selected as Territorial Governor. After Arizona became a state in 1912, George was elected Governor 7 times. Duett was a gracious, confident first lady. She was loved by all of Arizona. They maintained homes in both Globe and Phoenix but Duett was always most comfortable at the Q Ranch in Pleasant Valley. She went there as often as she could.

In April of 1931, their only daughter, Virginia, gave birth to their first grandchild, a baby boy. Less than one week later Duett died of complications from a ruptured appendix. She was 63. George was shocked and saddened at the death of Duett. He became despondent and was not able to concentrate on the upcoming election. He died in late December of 1934. His death was attributed to heart disease, but friends said that he lost strength because of Duett's death and the loss of the election in 1934.

BEAR HOWARD 1817-1910

It is hard to find anyone who came to the Arizona Territory who is more colorful or more of a character than Bear Howard. His arrival in Arizona was not so much of his own desire or planned far in advance. When you are running from the law, the Arizona Territory was always a good option. Bear found himself in that predicament after killing a Mexican sheepherder over a grazing dispute. His daughter, Martha, got him out of jail by baking a file into a "birthday cake" she sent to him. After his escape, friends in law enforcement encouraged him to move. Bear, along with the entire family headed to Arizona. Bear got his name from the large number of bears he had killed. This was one of his primary means of livelihood. Whether feeding hungry miners in California or hungry lumber men in Arizona, Bear Howard found that bear meat is tasty and one bear will go a long way!

In the 1880's he built a little cabin using sandstone rock in Oak Creek Canyon, where the West Fork hiking trail is today. His family, including son Jesse and daughter Martha, along with her husband Stephen Purtymun and their ever growing family, eventually nine children, joined him in the canyon.

Bear was an enormous man. At 6' 6" tall he towered over most men. He was also incredibly strong and powerfully built. He had a hot temper and a personality that was larger than life. Put all these things together and you have the stuff that legends are made of. Although Bear had died by the time my Dad was born in 1914, my Dad spoke of him often, as the stories about him persisted for decades. My Dad wrote about him in some of his stories and recounts the fights he would get into in Flagstaff, and how, even in his seventies, he could "whip just about anyone."

Bear had been a widower for many years when he tried marriage again. He married Elizabeth Ragsdale James, widow of another Oak Creek Canyon pioneer. The marriage lasted only three months. Elizabeth was "tired of the smelly hound dogs lying around the house." Bear, not making any adjustments in the housing arrangement apparently chose the dogs.

Bear was in remarkably good health and lived to be 93. He spent the last years of his life living with his daughter Martha and her second husband, James Cook in Yeager Canyon near Prescott.

Bear Howard, standing center, with his hound dogs, 2 bears, and a group of Flagstaff locals. Photo courtesy of Sedona Heritage Museum.

To find out more about Bear Howard, and his family, read the wonderful story of Martha "Mattie" Purtymun in my book, "Three Cheers for Unbreakable Dolls".

BIG MINNIE AND JOE BIGNON

The famous Bird Cage Theater in Tombstone, Arizona was originally built to offer "respectable entertainment" to women and families. It did not appeal to the respectable families in Tombstone and not a single respectable woman ever entered its doors in all its years of operation. It quickly became a haven for the red light women, miners, heavy drinking, gun toting gamblers, and an occasional cowboy.

It changed hands a number of times over the years but by far one of the most colorful owners were Big Minnie and her husband Joe Bignon. Big Minnie ran the Bird Cage wearing a number of different hats depending on the need of the hour. She was a madam, a prostitute, an actress and when needed, the bouncer. On one occasion, the bartender, Charley Keene was trying to deal with an unruly customer, upset over the price of whiskey. He called out for someone to fetch the Marshall. "We don't need the Marshall," Big Minnie exclaimed, "I'll throw him out myself!" and she did.

Her husband Joe was apparently in charge of the marketing and advertising for the Bird Cage. He sent out handbills which described his wife as, "230 pounds of loveliness in pink tights."

When gold was discovered in nearby Pearce the Bignon's moved there and opened Joe Bignon's Palace. They remained there until their deaths and are buried in the Pearce, now a ghost town, cemetery.

Ed Tewksbury

Edwin was born in 1858 in San Francisco, California. The second son of J.D. Tewksbury, who hailed from Maine, and his beautiful Indian wife whose name is unknown to this day. The Tewksburys came to the Arizona Territory in the early 1880's. By this time the mother had died leaving 5 children, 4 boys and a girl. They were horse people but when they came upon beautiful and very isolated Pleasant Valley they began to raise cattle along with their horses.

When not hunting, working the ranch, training horses or killing those involved in the feud, Ed Tewksbury dressed well and was meticulously groomed, circa 1880's.

The "good looking Tewksbury boys" would have gone into oblivion as so many pioneer families did had they not become involved in America's most deadly family feud, the Pleasant Valley War. It is estimated 30 to 50 men were killed during this feud over a period of several violent and stormy years. Ed Tewksbury, a crack shot, was responsible for a number of the killings.

The Pleasant Valley War was also one of the reasons Arizona was denied statehood. On August 1, 1892, Ed, the only surviving Tewksbury, was seen purchasing fruit in Pleasant Valley. On August 2nd, at 5 a.m., Tom Graham, the only surviving Graham brother, was shot in the back as he was delivering a load of wheat to the flour mill in Tempe, Arizona. Tom Graham was still alive and named Ed Tewksbury and John Rhodes as his assailants. John Rhodes had married the widow of John Tewksbury who had been ambushed and killed by Tom Graham. Tom Graham lived for three days, paralyzed from the chest down. Every few hours he would ask his wife Annie to rub his stomach hoping the feeling would come back. After his death, Ed Tewksbury and John Rhodes were arrested. On the opening day of the trial Annie Graham pulled a pistol to shoot Ed and John, but it caught on her dress before she could fire. Hysterical, she was removed from the courtroom. John Rhodes was released immediately as many vouched that he was at a hotel in Tempe when the shooting occurred. Ed spent time in prison and went through two trials. Ed was acquitted for the simple reason that it was deemed IMPOSSIBLE for a man to ride 75 miles one way over the roughest terrain imaginable in 18 hours, then ride back again!

After his release from prison, he happened to pass by the camp of the Lopez family whom he did not know. He "took a shine" to their daughter, Braulia and basically carried her off and married her. When she asked her parents why they let him take her they replied, "We were terrified of him." Ed and Braulia settled in Globe, Arizona where he was respected and elected constable for two terms. He also served as the Deputy Sheriff for Gila County.

Four children 3 boys and a girl were born in rapid succession. Edwin Tewksbury died from complications of tuberculosis, which had plagued the family, in 1904. Two months later his last son was born. The baby was named George Wilson Tewksbury, after the George Wilson in the photo on the front cover.

Epilogue

Who killed Tom Graham? Before his death, Ed confessed to his step mother that he indeed had killed Tom Graham. He had a string of horses lined up from Pleasant Valley to Tempe and "rode like the devil." His primary horse was his legendary stallion, Sockwad. This story was confirmed by Mary Ann Tewksbury Rhodes who told her children late in her life "Uncle Ed killed Tom Graham to keep Papa (John Rhodes) from doing it." John Rhodes was also present at the shooting. After making himself very visible at the hotel; he made a brief excursion out to meet Ed. How did they get away with it? Frontier justice and the Tewksburys had a lot of friends.

Read the wonderful story of Mary Ann Tewksbury and life in Pleasant Valley, in "Unbreakable Dolls, Too".

THE PLEASANT VALLEY WAR

Pleasant Valley, even today, is extremely isolated. Located on the rugged Mogollon Rim, mountains, steep canyons and dense forests make the area even now a formidable place. Pleasant Valley was 70 miles from Globe, 70 miles from Holbrook and 90 miles from Prescott, as the crow flies, but they weren't flying, they traveled over hard and difficult trails, on horses or wagons making the journey much more difficult. The Tewksbury family staked a claim on land in Pleasant Valley in 1878.

A short time later while in Globe, John Tewksbury invited the Graham brothers to Pleasant Valley. There was plenty of land, grass as far as the eye could see and a steady supply of fresh water. It would be nice to have neighbors. The Tewksburys and the Grahams were friends, helping one another build their cabins. They also went in together to form a joint herd of cattle. When the Grahams tried to persuade the Tewksburys to rustle cattle from other settlers in the area, the Tewksburys refused, saying they wouldn't steal from their neighbors. This created tension between the two families but they continued to build the herd of cattle and forged a brand together.

Tom Graham and John Tewksbury headed to Prescott to register the brand. Prescott was 90 miles away, a long, arduous journey even today. In the late 1800's it took several days, one way. John Graham told them he had to go to Prescott anyway, he would be happy to register the brand for them and save them the trip. In Prescott, the Territorial Capital, John Graham registered the brand in the Graham name ONLY. He effectively rustled the Tewksbury share of cattle right out from under them.

The Pleasant Valley War was on! Murders, lynchings, vigilante groups, posses, inquests, trials and juries became all to familiar to the residents of Pleasant Valley. It became a terrifying place to live. Lawmen from every direction were involved, such notables as Commodore Perry Owens, Sheriff of Apache County, Sheriff Mulvenon of Prescott and William "Bucky" O'Neil.

Men disappeared, their bodies never found. Men were found murdered on the trails leading in and out of Pleasant Valley, no one knew who they were or if it was related to the war. Prized animals were also killed. It was America's most deadly feud, far surpassing the more well known "Hatfield and McCoy" feud, lasting more than a decade.

It is often reported as a cattle vs. sheep range war, but the Tewksburys took sheep on shares two years after the feud began, an aggravating factor, but not the cause of the feud. The exact death toll will never be known, the best estimates are between 20 and 30. It devastated not only the Tewksburys and the Grahams but many other families as well. No women were killed, but they were still victims, losing husbands, fathers and sons. Numerous books have been written and then made for television. In 1992, the movie, "Gunsmoke, to the Last Man" is a depiction of the Pleasant Valley War.

For more information on the Pleasant Valley War: "The Pleasant Valley War" by Jinx Pyle, "A Little War of Our Own" by Don Dedera

The Yuma Territorial Prison, aka "Hell Hole" 1885-1909

Hell Hole is an accurate nickname for this horrid place. Arizona had many homegrown outlaws to populate the prison. The last territory to become a state had a reputation as a great place for an outlaw to hole up. So with the great geographical advantage to hide, there was an incentive for many from all over the globe to migrate here. It was easy to get lost in the Arizona Territory with all the other murderers, robbers, thieves and scoundrels.

It was built at a cost of $25,000. In this arid desert land, the only materials available for construction were local rock and handmade adobe bricks. Once the prison was up and running, the labor for the many additions to house more prisoners, came from the current prisoners serving time. With the mighty and then untamed Colorado running on one side, the Gila River on the other and surrounded by the Sonoran Desert it was not an easy place to escape. It was considered the "Alcatraz of the Desert." Yuma was isolated, with Tucson 220 miles of desert to the east, and San Diego 170 miles of desert to the west. Armed guards were everywhere and they would shoot first, ask questions later. In the summer temperatures rose to 120 during the day. In the winter, it could become brutally cold, especially at night.

The prisoners were packed, 6 to a cell. Each 8 foot by 9 foot cell contained two tiers of bunks, three bunks to each tier, no wider than 18 inches. The steel bunks had a skimpy straw tick mattress and one blanket. There was not a wash basin or toilet facilities. Only a bucket, which was emptied once daily. Think about it. 120 degree heat, 6 men, one bucket. Multiply that by many cells of six men each.

Inside of the prison was the dreaded, "Snake Den." So named for the rattlesnakes that seemed to find their way in. Prison officials insisted that the snakes, "just came in", but prisoners insisted that the guards intentionally dropped them in. The den was hollowed out of solid rock. It was 10x10 with only a tiny hole at the top for a minimum of ventilation. This was solitary confinement. The room was totally bare except for a chain that the prisoner was shackled to. No blanket, no mattress, not even a bucket. The men used one corner of the room. Water and one small loaf of bread was delivered daily. No companionship except a rattlesnake or scorpion. Some with fatal results.

Some of the guards were descent sorts and humane. Unfortunately, prisons always attract brutal, abusive, and sadistic men as prison guards. One of the worst was a man by the name of Shreeves. He would taunt, and poke at men, nearly driving them crazy. He would work them till they dropped. He would beat them every chance he got. One day he was out in the yard supervising, and alternately, beating four men. Finally, the four men had enough and attacked him. Shreeves was dead! In desperation the four tried to come up with a plan. They had been in the process of building bricks for a wall. They quickly grabbed his body, placed it on the wall, and covered it with brick and mortar. A wall in the prison yard had never gone up so fast! When Schreeves replacement arrived, he commended the men for the excellent work on the wall and inquired of them where Schreeves was. "We don't know, he just left and never came back." Inquiries were made around the prison and then around Yuma. No one had seen him. The prison guards continued to ask the four men and they stuck to their same simple story. The prison assumed he had marriage troubles and had left town. No one seemed to really care. No one liked him.

As you can imagine in a horrible place like this, prison breaks were attempted frequently. Prison guards were overpowered and their guns stolen. Then all pandemonium would break out. On one of these attempts, three guards had been killed including the guard manning the Gatling, the armed tower that overlooked the prison. Escape seemed certain. Gunfire came from the Gatling again! In disbelief the prisoners looked up to see the pretty wife of the prison superintendent at the Gatling manning the gun. One prisoner exclaimed, "Good Grief! It's Mrs. Ingalls!" The prisoners had great respect for Mrs. Ingalls. She had opened a library, improved the living conditions for the men and even supplied them with treats from her own kitchen. She had taught literacy to any who wanted to learn. How she got there, and how she knew how to operate the gun, no one knew. All the prisoners froze. You don't shoot a woman! Suddenly one prisoner, less chivalrous than the others screamed, "Shoot her you fools! What are you waiting for?" With chivalry out the door, gunfire erupted, but Dora Ingalls remained unscathed. With her constant gunfire, the prisoners were unable to escape and within the hour, things were under control.

This was the dreadful fate that waited lawbreakers at Arizona Territorial Prison in Yuma. In the years of operation the prison held a total of 3,069 people, including 29 women. It averaged less than one successful escape every year (26). 111 died while at the prison, mostly from Tuberculosis.

THE COWBOYS ON THE COVER

I love this picture. As a matter of fact, I love this picture so much I have a copy of it hanging over my kitchen sink. It was taken in 1884 and was featured in an Arizona magazine that would later be called, Arizona Highways. Bill Brown, a Tewksbury descendent who has two relatives in the picture told me that it is staged photo. The white horse in the background is not a living horse, possibly taxidermy special. The cowboys are playfully bantering their guns and one has a noose around another's neck. In reality, these men were the real deal. Many were famous already in Arizona but within the next 20 years all of them would be well known in Arizona and throughout the West. Within two short years most of them would be fully involved in the Pleasant Valley War, America's most deadly family feud between the Tewksburys and the Grahams.

From left to right, standing, Ed Tewksbury, George Wilson, Charlie Meadows, Tom Horn, Jim Tewksbury. Kneeling: John Rhodes, Carter Hazelton, Jim Roberts, Jim Houck. 1884. Courtesy of Gila County Historical Museum.

ED TEWKSBURY

The fascinating story of Ed is featured on page 74.

George Wilson

If George Wilson looks like he about 14, it's because he is 14. How this young man managed to wrangle his way into this elite photo opp with famous cowboys is beyond me. I imagine that George's parents had money, influence or friends in high places to arrange such a feat. George went on to become a successful banker in Globe.

Charlie Meadows

The Meadows family made quite the first impression when they arrived in Payson in the spring of 1877. They came with 6 huge wagons, loaded down with goods and supplies. Hundreds of horses and cattle accompanied them.

The Meadows arrived with 8 of their 12 children, including 17 year-old Charlie. They started their Diamond Valley Ranch not far from Payson. Life was good for the family until Apaches killed the father and brother.

In 1884, Charlie was instrumental in helping start the Payson Rodeo, which continues on to this day. There, he put his roping and riding skills to good use. Going by the name of "Arizona" Charlie Meadows he went into the Wild West Show Business. He traveled all over the United States and to Australia, Europe, Asia and Alaska. While in Australia, he met a young girl who had run away from home to join the Wild West Show. A romance was sparked and continued on board ship and eventually led to marriage. Unfortunately, the marriage didn't last and Charlie continued doing shows. He rubbed shoulders with such famous celebrities as Buffalo Bill Cody, Annie Oakley, Will Rogers and Jack London.

Later in life he came to Yuma and became the largest landholder in Yuma County. He focused his attention on his ranch and devoted himself to a fond relationship with his daughter, Marion, whom he did not meet until she was an adult.

Charlie Meadows died in 1932 and is buried in Yuma, Arizona.

Tom Horn 1860-1903

No one in history had a higher opinion of himself than
Tom Horn. Embellishment, exaggeration and continuing
reassessment of the facts characterized Tom's life. Born in
Memphis, Missouri in the tumultuous year of 1860 he was
raised in a farm family of 4 boys and 4 girls. At 14, Tom ran
away from home and headed West, on foot. He managed
most days to get fed by some sympathetic farm wife. He took odd jobs
here and there as he traveled.

Within a year he had arrived in Arizona and was working near the
Verde River. By that time he was no longer on foot, but had earned
enough to buy a good horse, saddle, bridle and a Winchester rifle. It wasn't
long before Tom and everyone else recognized his gift for languages. He
quickly learned Spanish. Al Sieber, famous frontiersman made Tom a
Government Scout and placed Tom among the Apache to live and work.
Tom quickly acclimated to this life learning the Apache language and their
ways. Tom would spend 15 years in Arizona. He was also a world class
rodeo champion and sometimes prospector. He became involved in the
Pleasant Valley War, but his role in the war was always murky. He was the
self-proclaimed mediator of the Pleasant Valley War. It was rumored that
he had been hired, to kill, by either the Grahams or the Tewksburys, but
no one was ever sure which side he was on. He was a hard drinker and
frequented the red light districts.

After his years as a government scout, interpreter, and prospector he
moved on to new occupations, that of a range regulator and hired killer
for the Pinkerton Detective Agency. Even in this he made himself virtu-
ous by viewing himself simply as "a dispenser of frontier justice." He also
took great pride that he notified his potential victims with the information
that they would be killed if they remained in the area. He also gave them
a decent amount of time, sometimes a month, to comply. Other victims
weren't so lucky. He used his tracking skills learned from the Apaches and
could track a man down; lie in wait for hours or days to kill him. The very
name or presence of Tom Horn brought reform to a community.

In July of 1903, he was accused of the murder of 14 year-old Willie Nickell. The one murder he did not commit. His on again, off again girlfriend, teacher Glendolene Kimmel, wrote a desperate letter to try to save him from hanging. Another friend wrote a petition of mercy relating a story of how Tom had saved the life of a young Apache boy, risking his own life in the process. Sheriff Cook of Albany County Wyoming described an incident "where he saw three little children in a railroad station dressed in rags. He (Tom) took them to a restaurant, fed them a hearty meal, and then bought them all a new set of clothes, including shoes as they were bare footed." Sheriff Cook added, "Don't tell me a man like that goes around killing children."

Yet on November 20, 1903, Tom Horn was hung. He was buried in Boulder, Colorado and had the biggest funeral the town had ever seen, with over 2,500 people in attendance. An armed guard was placed at his grave.

JIM TEWKSBURY 1860-1888

Jim Tewksbury was a crack shot and known as "the deadliest of the Tewksburys". He was of course, a participant of the Pleasant Valley War, but he did not die from gunshot wounds. The Tewksbury family had been plagued with a propensity to Tuberculosis. He died in Phoenix at the age of 28. He had been staying at the home of his sister, Elvira Slosser, who had been caring for him.

JOHN RHODES

The Tewksbury family had the most devoted, loyal and faithful friend in the person of John Rhodes. He first appears in Pleasant Valley about the same time as the Grahams and Tewksburys. He had a Mexican girlfriend, Trinidad Lopez. Together they had three children. When the Pleasant Valley War heated up, Trinidad returned to her actual husband and other children in Mexico, where it was safer.

John Rhodes eventually married Mary Ann Tewksbury, the widow of John Tewksbury who had been shot from behind by Tom Graham not far from their cabin. In addition to marriage in December of 1888, they combined five children all under the age of five. John and Mary Ann would go on to have six more children together.

They remained in Pleasant Valley continuing ranching and raising their family. In the early 1900's they moved to Southern Arizona where they ranched near Mammoth.

At age 55, John Rhodes was the oldest man to serve with the Arizona Rangers. He died in 1919 at age 68.

CARTER HAZELTON

Carter Hazelton was the oldest son of 6 children. He came from Virginia to homestead near Payson with his 5 younger siblings and widowed mother, Obedience.

The Meadows family and the Hazelton family were friends. Carter's sister Sarah, "was sweet on" Henry Meadows. Sarah was devastated when Henry was killed by Apaches at the Meadows Diamond Valley Ranch.

Carter was also involved in the Pleasant Valley War. He married Mattie Stewart and together they had 8 children. Their first son, Lewis, was killed in World War I and buried in France. The family homesteaded along the Gila River. They became prominent citizens of Buckeye.

JIM ROBERTS

Jim Roberts was born in 1859 in Missouri. His family came to the Arizona Territory and homesteaded in Green Valley, present day Payson. His love of fine horses is what drew Jim and Ed Tewksbury together and was the basis for their lasting friendship. By the mid 1880's he was up to his eyeballs in the Pleasant Valley War. In 1889, he married Amelia Kirkland from Congress, Arizona. They would have 6 children together, 4 boys and 2 girls.

That same year he was appointed Deputy Sheriff to the famous Bucky O'Neil, Sheriff of Yavapai County. He would remain in law enforcement for the remainder of his life. He would serve as Deputy Sheriff, Constable, Marshall, and mine watchman. In an article in the Arizona Republic, it was stated:

> Jim Roberts, the company's police force is a terror to evildoers. Roberts gets $300.00 a month. His duties include collections for electric light service. He is in demand elsewhere, but prefers Jerome.

At the age of 70, and still working, Jim single-handedly killed one and captured another bank robber in a spectacular display of marksmanship in Clarkdale. He was considered Arizona's premier gun fighter.

He died in 1934 on the streets of Clarkdale of a heart attack at age 75.

Jim Houck

This is the same Jim Houck who is mentioned in the John Shaw story. He was the Sheriff of Apache County, with Holbrook being the County Seat. It is said of him, "He thought nothing of taking a life if it suited his purpose." This could be the reason the cowboys in the John Shaw story hated him so much.

Chet Houck, Jim's brother, was the beloved Sheriff of Navajo County, Winslow being the County Seat. Chet Houck is also featured in the John Shaw story. It was said of him, that "he was the antithesis of his brother Jim."

Along with being a Sheriff, Jim Houck ran sheep. Toward the end of his life he suffered business reverses. One morning, after feeding the chickens, he told his family he had taken strychnine because "he was tired of living." He lay down on the bed and asked that his shoes be removed and that is how he died.

Dennis McDonald

Dennis, age 4

You might be thinking, "All the colorful characters lived 100 years ago, there is no one that colorful now." Not so. There is no one as colorful as my own brother-in-law, Dennis McDonald.

"Break it!" Were some of Dennis' first words as a tiny toddler. Not only did he say it, he did it! Nothing was safe and many things were destroyed. He wasn't malicious, just curious as to how things worked, and how would you know how things worked if you didn't get a chance to look inside? Sometimes Dennis' most profitable hours were at night when everyone was sleeping. One night they woke up to find Dennis in the kitchen playing with knives. Concerned about his safety, his parents "locked" him in his crib by placing a board on top and securing with a latch. Dennis outwitted them and pulled up the mattress and escaped through the springs.

Fire was another thing that fascinated Dennis. He loved to watch things burn. After setting several fires, including the curtains in his sister's room, his parents were very concerned. Child psychology was new in the 1950's and Dennis was the perfect candidate. The psychologist prescribed setting fire to one of his favorite toys to break him of what was becoming a very bad habit. His parents got his favorite teddy bear, and with Dennis watching, they threw the bear into the fireplace. Dennis stood transfixed while the bear burned. Then he took off running. His parents looked at each other and smiled. It worked! Their enthusiasm was short lived when Dennis returned with an armload of toys, dropped them at their feet and said, "Fire!"

The most serious fire occurred years later when half of their free standing garage burned to the ground. The fire started at night and was a three alarm fire. Although Dennis readily admitted he had started the other house fires, he stood his ground for decades that he was NOT the culprit that started the garage fire. He maintained that this was the one time he was innocent. One day Dennis and I were talking in the kitchen and the subject of the fires came up. Dennis once again proclaimed his innocence. I said, "So Dennis, let's go over what happened that day." Dennis replied, "Well, I was out in the garage that morning. I had hidden some money in a straw mattress that was out there and I wanted to check to see if it was still there. The light in the garage wasn't working so I lit a match. I was there in the morning; the fire didn't start till that night." I couldn't believe what I was hearing, "Dennis! You DID start that fire! Fires smolder for hours before they really take off." Dennis was surprised by this new revelation, but he accepted it. After all he had done, what was one more thing?

Dennis had been born with a number of undiagnosed learning disabilities. In the 1950's these were all lumped under one umbrella, "he's got ants in his pants." School was very difficult and he was passed from grade to grade mostly because the teachers didn't want to deal with him for another year. He fondly remembers high school as "the best 8 years of my life."

He was finally asked to leave high school after participating in his 5th senior prank. Flagstaff High School colors were green and brown. Dennis and his friends had obtained brown paint and painted the doors to the school closed so you could not enter or exit. They had also painted on the walkways, "74' HAS MORE." The police were fairly certain of their suspects and brought Dennis and his friend into the police station for questioning. They were even more certain when they saw the brown paint on the boys pants. The officers were having a hard time being serious as all four had also graduated from Flagstaff High School and had participated in their own senior pranks. The officers took turns interrogating these two comedians. Finally one of the officers pointed at the paint on the boys pants and said, "What color is that paint?" "Well," Dennis replied, "it's not a light brown, it's not a dark brown, it's a Joe Brown." Joe Brown was the principal at Flagstaff High School. The officers fled the room and closed the door as quickly as they could but not before the boys heard all four of them erupt in laughter.

Out of high school but without a diploma and no way to pass the GED, Dennis began looking for work. His ability to fix things landed him a job at a local car wash. No matter what broke or went wrong, Dennis was able to fix it. In his spare time he was driving too fast, drinking, getting in fights, smoking, womanizing, and doing some drugs.

It was at this time that I became a Christian. I had married his brother two years earlier. Dennis had painted the "Just Married" sign on our vehicle but it was spelled, "just marred." I tried to talk to Dennis about how he needed to become a Christian and that Jesus would help him with his many problems. Dennis never had to be convinced that he was a sinner! He listened but resisted. One day he came to me so pleased with himself I thought he was going to burst. He said he had a great idea. "I do want to get saved, the popular term in the 70's, just not right now. I am going to wait till right before I die and then I will get saved." I pointed out the obvious problems with this idea but to no avail. Two months later Dennis and his friend were returning from a trip to Lake Powell. He and his friend had been drinking and driving a GTO home across the reservation at 110 miles an hour. As they topped a hill, below them was a flock of sheep in the road. Always the optimist, Dennis turned to his friend and said, "At least they're not cows." Both boys closed their eyes and just like the parting of the Red Sea, the sheep moved half to the left and half to the right and they sailed right through not hitting a single one. As Dennis related this story he looked at me sheepishly, no pun intended, and said, "I forgot to get saved." From then on Dennis was more attentive.

One evening he heard the testimony of an equally notorious local by the name of Tommy Eickmeyer. Everyone who knew Tommy had seen a dramatic and miraculous change. In December of 1978, Dennis took the plunge. Gone was the drinking, the drugs, even the smoking. He quit overnight, never having another cigarette. But Dennis was still Dennis, and the fun and laughter continued, although in a new vein.

Dennis had severe dyslexia and had never learned to read. His desire to know and understand the Bible had been a motivating factor in helping him learn to read. Dennis married a beautiful girl, Susie Hicks, whom he met at church. For a time they pastored churches in South Dakota and Missouri. Even during his sermons, the dyslexia could kick in and Susie sometimes had difficulty keeping a straight face. During one sermon, Dennis was talking about the cleansing of the lepers, but he called it the cleansing of the leopards. Serious health problems brought them back to Flagstaff. Getting a job was difficult; he still didn't have a diploma or a GED.

Dennis heard about a job opportunity with Dick Cook. Dick had a small manufacturing business where they were making oars for canoes. Dan Cook, the owner's son also worked there. Dan had been in high school with Dennis. Dennis, it seemed, had been in school at one time or another with just about everyone. Dan remembered his time with Dennis in high school and told his father, "I don't think this is a good idea."

Dennis started at Quintus making canoe oars. Dick thought he was doing well, so he took him to Camp Verde where they were making wind turbines. Dennis continued to do well and Dick advanced him to floor supervisor then to general supervisor. It was at this time that Dennis' engineering genius came to light. He could fix anything, he could look at a project and know what needed to be done, how to do it, how to make it better and how to make it faster. He also could invent things. With no formal training it was just how his mind worked.

The company was expanding making medical, defense, and military products. Dennis had a way with working with people, placing people in positions where they were happy and most productive. They also hired engineers and Dennis said, "I hire people smarter than me." During these early years, there were a number of El Salvadorians leaving the political unrest in their country. Dick hired them and Dennis trained them. They hired entire families so that people could stay together. Dennis couldn't remember their names so he began calling them, Jose, Hose B and Hose C. They were not at all offended because they knew Dennis cared about them and they loved him! Many co-workers became Christians while working with him at Quintus. Here they were able to get a good job and get established in the country.

After 18 years, Dennis finally got his diploma from Flagstaff High School. He was so proud! During business or project meetings with a room full of engineers. Dennis, now President and COO, would start by saying, "I'm not an engineer, but I think we should do it this way or try that way." The engineers were shocked at his ingenuity and creative ideas and say, "Where did you go to school?" They surely thought he was joking when he proudly answered that he was a graduate of Flagstaff High School and "The School of Hard Knocks."

Quintus grew to a multi-million dollar company employing a large number of people in the Verde Valley. Dick and Dennis wanted to use the profits to help many local organizations in the Verde Valley as well as worldwide missions organizations.

Dennis was happy. He had a beautiful wife and two beautiful children. He had a comfortable home on two acres of land. He enjoyed his work. He was involved in his church. What more could a man want?

The McDonald family, left to right, Dennis, Susie, Megan, daughter-in-law Camille, and Jason.

There was something missing. Dennis found it in an alter ego! One afternoon at a family get together Dennis casually remarked that he had run into a distant cousin and that cousin might be dropping by. He told us that the cousin was "back woods" and we should really try our best to show him kindness. Sure enough, in the middle of the afternoon there was a knock at the door and in barged someone claiming to be Harley Hall and wasn't he "Jest so happy to git to meet up with all his relatives." Oh boy what a sight! Grey stringy hair to his shoulders, big yellow buck teeth that had been manufactured just for Harley, ratty clothes, a sad looking hat and a rather blank stare. This was the new found cousin. It was hard to know what to watch, Harley working the crowd or the family and friends trying to be polite. Harley began making regular, unannounced appearances and you never knew where he might show up. It could be at a wedding, a birthday party, a business event or an international airport.

One memorable Thanksgiving, his niece Lisa, was bringing the entire Ball State Girls' basketball team to his house to celebrate. The team would be playing in a tournament the next day at Northern Arizona University. Most of the girls had never been west of the Mississippi and they were so excited to see the Grand Canyon and get a glimpse of life in Arizona. As the big tour bus pulled into the street, who should come out to meet the bus but none other than Harley Hall himself! He waved down the bus,

Infamous "Harley Hall" entertains at a family gathering.

forcing it to stop in the middle of the street. He stepped into the bus and said, "Well howdy girls! I been waitin' for ya. I got all the trash burned up in them burn barrels in the back yard to git it all cleaned up nice for ya. I been out huntin' all mornin' and I got me two nice skunks, got em' cookin' for ye right now. You all jest come in now and make yourselves to home." There was dead silence on the bus. Lisa turned around to sneak a peek at their reaction. It was hard for her not to laugh at the total shock and disbelief on their faces. Of course Dennis took off his get up so "they could see how handsome I am." He and Susie then treated them to a first class Thanksgiving dinner, for among his other talents, he is a gourmet cook. That next spring while visiting Muncie, Indiana, I asked the girls what they enjoyed most about their trip to Arizona. It wasn't the Grand Canyon or wining the NAU basketball tournament. It was unanimous, "Coach Mac's Uncle Dennis!"

Dennis McDonald, a true colorful character and a scoundrel who became a saint.

Acknowledgements

Climax Jim

The Outrageous Climax Jim, True West Article, November 5, 2012 by Marshall Trimble. Climax Jim: The Tumultuous Tale of Arizona's Rustling Cowboy, Karen Holliday Tanner and John D. Tanner Jr. Graham County/Arizona Territory Show and Tell. Find a Grave memorial/Nancy Brown. Various other sources

Larcena Pennington

Stalwart Women, by Leo Banks, 1999, Book Division of Arizona Highways.

Charles Sterling and Richard Wilson

Oral history from Paul Thompson, grandson of Oak Creek Canyon's first settler, Jim Thompson.

Sarah Bowman

Stalwart Women, by Leo Banks, 1999, Book Division of Arizona Highways. Arizona Nuggets, Dean Smith, 2009, Historic Arizona Press. Various other books, and articles.

George Kirk

Author's personal history of the Kirk family, Flagstaff Historian Jerry Snow, oral history, Navajo Code Talker display at Burger King in Kayenta, various articles.

John Shaw

Thanks to local historian Jerry Snow, for the information, oral history and articles about John Shaw. Article, Arizona Highways Magazine, A Drink for the Dead, June 1963 by Gladwell Richardson.

Clara Penny

Thanks to Dave and Barbara Penny for their remembrance of Dave's grandmother, Clara Penny. Also for all photos that contributed to this story.

Alvin Booth

Thanks to the always helpful volunteers at the Gila County Museum for the story, articles and information about Alvin Booth.

Gabrielle "Dollie" Wiley

Thanks to Sedona Historian Linda Star for her help and information on this story. Leo W. Banks, article, August 12,1999 , A Madam, A Murder a Mystery. Speaking Ill of the Dead, Jerks in Arizona, Sam Lowe, 2012, Globe Pequot Press, Guilford, Connecticut

GLEN AND BESSIE HYDE

Sunk Without a Sound, Brad Dimock, 2001, Fretwater Press, Flagstaff, Arizona. Over the Edge: Death in Grand Canyon, Michael P. Ghiglieri, Thomas M. Myers, Puma Press, Flagstaff, Arizona (Authors Note: Tom Myers is brother to Dave Myers included in the Dedication at the beginning of the book) Numerous friends who have done extensive hiking and/ or river rafting in the Grand Canyon.

FRED KABOTIE

Thanks to Ed Kabotie and his sister Meg, for their remembrance of their great-grand father, Fred Kabotie. Painted Desert Inn, Petrified Forest National Park. Fred Kabotie: Hopi Indian Artist, Fred Kabotie with Bill Bellknap, 1977, Museum of Northern Arizona/Northland Press, Flagstaff, Arizona.

CHARLIE ALLEN

Thanks to Paul Thompson, grandson of first settler, Jim Thompson, for his amazing and wonderful stories about Oak Creek Canyon and Sedona!

AMANDA "JUDGE" MILLER

Thanks to Vincent Ritchie for his remembrance and information about a long lost relative! Ex slave interview/ Annie Lee Newton, research worker, Federal Writers Project, Athens Georgia, 1937.

HADJI ALI/HI JOLLY

Thanks to one of the premier experts on the 1857 Beale Expedition, historian Jerry Snow for his information regarding Hi Jolly. The Journal of Arizona History, Volume 49 #2 Summer, 2005 Gary Paul Nabhan.

CLYDE TOMBAUGH

Thanks to the marvelous staff at Lowell Observatory for information about Clyde Tombaugh. Clyde Tombaugh Discoverer of Pluto, David H. Levy, 1991 University of Arizona Press. Clyde Tombaugh and the Search for Planet X, Margaret K. Wetterer, 1996 Carolrhoda Books, Minneapolis, Minnesota.

JENNIE BAUTER

Thanks to Linda Star, Sedona Historian for her information about Jennie Bauter. Linda has done many presentations about Arizona Women. Mohave Museum of History, Mohave Memories, July 2014.

HERMANN WOLF

Thanks to Jerry Snow for taking me to see the Canyon Diablo Trading Post to see Hermann Wolf's grave. Thanks to Jerry for his information about Hermann Wolf. Article, Mystery Surrounds Wolf Post Founder, Toni Richardson, Arizona Days and Ways, September 15, 1957.

Damacia Baca
Oral history from pioneer families in the White Mountains, Holbrook Historical Museum, other sources.

Helen Duett Hunt
Gila County Historical Society, Globe, Arizona. Helen Duett Ellison Hunt: Arizona's first FIRST Lady, Mary Brown, The Print Raven, Flagstaff, Arizona.

Bear Howard
So many people have given me great stories about Bear Howard! First my Dad, Verner G. Benson, Purtymun family members, the Pendley family, Paul Thompson, and Sedona Historical Museum.

Big Minnie and Joe Bignon
Hell's Belles of Tombstone, Ben Traywick, 1993

The Arizona Territorial Prison at Yuma
My primary source of information was a book given to me a few years ago by a Yuma native. The Hell Hole: The Yuma Prison Story, William and Milarde Brent, 1962. This husband and wife team wrote this interesting , although it gave me nightmares, book after interviewing a number of people who had either been in prison there, worked there, or were some other way associated with the prison. They present the prisoners side of the story. The State of Arizona has quite a different stance stating that: "It was humanely administered and was a model institution for its time. Schooling was available as well as a library and a hospital."

Cowboys on the Cover
Thanks to Donna Anderson and her fabulous staff at the Gila County Museum in Globe, Arizona for much of the information. Also, thanks to Bill Brown, John Rhodes and Mary Bryce, all Tewksbury descendants for their valuable, delightful and very entertaining input. Thanks to Wilma Haught of the Perkins Store Museum in Young, Arizona. Books: The Pleasant Valley War, Jinx Pyle, 2009, They Shot Billy Today, Leland J. Hanchett, 2006, A Little War of Our Own, Don Dedera, 1988. Excellent articles by Jayne Peace Pyle.

Dennis McDonald
Last, but never least. Thanks to my beloved brother in law, Dennis, better than any real brother ever could have been! Fortunately for me, I was witness to, or heard first hand of most of these escapades. Thank you Dennis for brightening all of our lives and being, oh so, COLORFUL!!!!

BOOKS BY JULIE MCDONALD

*All books are available as eBooks for .99 cents on book selling websites
*Print books are available at various Arizona retailers or
through Amazon for $10.00*

Arizona and Pioneer History

- Unbreakable Dolls (2012)*
- Unbreakable Dolls, Too (2013)*
- Three Cheers for Unbreakable Dolls (2014)*
- Saints & Scoundrels: Colorful Characters of the American West (2014)
- Saints & Scoundrels: Colorful Characters of Arizona (2015)*
- Saints & Scoundrels: Colorful Characters of Grand Canyon (April 2017)*

Gardening

- Farm Your Front Yard (*2012, 2014)
- Growing and Selling Your Produce and Flowers (2016)
- Perennials: Forever Friends (2017)
- How I made a Million Dollars Selling Pot(s) (2017)

Single Story eBooks

Concise, 20–40 pages, with great historic photos as well as contemporary color photos

- The 1931 Trunk Murders: The Story of Winnie Ruth Judd (2015)
- Elizabeth Heiser: Cattle Rancher & Cougar (2015)
- Clara Brown: The Rags to Riches Story of a Freed Slave (2016)
- Honeymoon Disappearance: Glen & Bessie Hyde's 1928 River Raft Trip Through Grand Canyon (2016)
- Philip Johnston and the Navajo Code Talkers (2016)
- Levi Coffin: President and Conductor on the Underground Railroad (2017)
- Arizona's Lovable Outlaw: The Escapades of Climax Jim (2017)

Christian eBooks

- Adventures in Giving (2014)
- Adventures in Freedom: 10 Steps to Forgiveness (2015)
- Adventures in Prayer (2015)
- Adventures in Caregiving (2016)
- Adventures in Simplicity (2017)
- Truth Behind the Tradition: Saint Nicholas (2016)
- Truth Behind the Tradition: Ireland's Saint Patrick (2016)

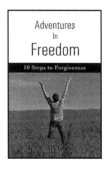